About the Author

John Birch was born in 1860 within the sound of Bow Bells. He had two sons and one daughter, and was married for sixty years. He established his own shop – J. B. Thomas & Sons: Tea, Coffee and Tobacco Merchants – at 'The Old Cigar Shop' in Kingston. The building still exists and the author is remembered by local people. He did not retire until in his seventies, and died in 1952.

The manuscript has been prepared for publication by Jean S. Moore, the author's granddaughter, who teaches nineteenth-century literature at Belmont Abbey College, North Carolina.

SHOP BOY

AN AUTOBIOGRAPHY

John Birch Thomas

CENTURY PUBLISHING

LONDON

First published in 1983 by
Routledge & Kegan Paul Plc

This edition published in 1985 by
Century Publishing Co. Ltd,
Portland House, 12–13 Greek Street,
London W1V 5LE

ISBN 0 7126 0840 0

The cover shows a painting by Louise Rayner

Reprinted in Great Britain by
Hunt Barnard Printing Ltd, Aylesbury, Bucks.

This book is in grateful memory of the late Captain Albert Larking, Secretary of the London Early Closing Association, whose indefatigable work for the amelioration of the conditions of shop workers' lives culminated in the passing of The Shops Act by the Right Honourable Winston Churchill in 1922.

CONTENTS

INTRODUCTION

When we were children, Friday was the day for tea at our grandparents' house in Kingston. Hot buttered crumpets and homemade cake were always on hand, but the real treat was Grandad's company. We would usually find him sitting at a high desk beside the fire and overlooking the French windows to his flower garden. He would be putting the finishing touches to his day's work on the autobiography he had waited to write until retirement in his seventies. Tea around the fire, or in the garden, meant hearing some of the latest anecdotes from the book, always told with humour and compassion.

Our grandfather was a self-educated and well-read man, enjoying a happy marriage for sixty years with his beloved Fanny Anne. They had three children, Tudor, Donald and Gwendolyn, and founded the tobacconist's shops of J. B. Thomas & Sons.

More than twenty-five years after Grandad died, when I was visiting England from my home in North Carolina, my brother, Mr John Sutherland of Kingston, suggested that Grandad's manuscript would be of interest in all areas of nineteenth-century studies. This being my own academic field, I offered to get the book typed in order to find a publisher. Our cousin, Miss Sally Thomas of Surbiton, the third grandchild, lent me the handwritten manuscript; I photocopied it in the United States, and the task began. It turned out to be necessary for me to type the work myself, because of the numerous Britishisms and archaic expressions, and the quirks of Grandad's handwriting, and so this job took two years.

As the stories from the book took shape on my typewriter, I could hear again Grandad's voice recounting his anecdotes by the fire, smoking his pipe and chuckling at the memories. I hope his readers will share in this pleasure.

Jean Sutherland Moore
Belmont Abbey College
North Carolina

PRELUDE

Apart from their surnames, none of the characters in this book is fictitious. It is a true account of actual happenings — a tale of memories crudely told. The book points no moral and its message — if any — is to record some of the conditions of shop life for some years before Mr Winston Churchill carried through his Shops Act in 1922.

So, if you are hard up for something to read and have patience to listen to him, Tom Lloyd will tell you of many things that happened after the rats came to the basement of an old house in Duke Street, West London, 'way back in the 1860s.

Had it not been for the rats the tale might have been quite different and he might not have met so many nice people, or the one he loved best of all.

So now I will withdraw and let the boy take up his tale and tell you (as far as possible in his own words) about life as he found it all those years ago.

J.B.T.

1

Before the rat came, I liked to play in the area* on fine mornings and look up at the people walking by, and wait until the cats-meat man came. Then I could put the meat in my wheelbarrow and go up and down shouting 'me-meat' like the man did, while Tibby followed me about and was given a little piece from time to time, until only the skewer was left. If it was raining, you had to do it in the breakfast room and down the long passage to the kitchen where Mother cooked things. When I wasn't taken out in the perambulator in the afternoon to St James's Park, I always played in the breakfast room.

Besides us, there were two gentlemen called 'the lodgers' living in our house. They had a lot of hair on their faces and were always in a hurry for their breakfast. They didn't have much time to talk to me, but they gave me pennies on Saturday. Father had a lot of hair too that tickled. He was very kind when he wasn't angry, and bought you wheelbarrows and gave you little bits of his bacon after you had finished your bread and milk. But Mother was the one who had most to say and brought in all the nice things to eat, so you couldn't help liking her best except sometimes when she washed you so much, and when she made you drink castor oil in milk when you weren't very well.

It was nice to be taken to the park in the afternoon and see the rows of cows outside the gates. You could get a glass

*Entrance to a basement door.

1

of new milk for a penny, or a little bowl of curds and whey. There were brown cows and some black, and one with black and white spots that Mother said was a piebald.

Inside the park we would go right round the pond and see the ducks and after that sit on a long seat with a lot of other young mothers with babies. They talked a lot and laughed, and used to look at the people going by and whisper things about them and then laugh again.

Sometimes tall soldiers came along with red jackets and little round hats on the side of their heads. Often they would stop and say, 'Good afternoon, Miss. Is that your first?' And the answer they got was, 'No, it's my second. The first is to come.' Then they would all laugh. It was nice to see them laugh — it made them look so happy and their eyes so kind.

Then, when you got tired of looking at them and shut your eyes, you found when you opened them again you were back again in the breakfast room with Tibby.

Sometimes after tea Uncle John came. He had long brown whiskers and was very strong. He could toss you up to the ceiling and put you on his shoulder and run up and down the area. He would get you on his knee and teach you to spell little words like m—a—t, mat. Then he would say, 'Eggsandbaconcabbageandfat — in four letters spell me that!' but I never could, so he would laugh and sometimes give me four pennies. Then Father and Uncle John would go out to a place they called the 'pubbly-kouse' and later on would come back with a big bottle, and you were taken upstairs to bed, but you couldn't sleep because of the laughing and talking that went on downstairs. Mother would sing about a dream she had about living in marble halls, and Uncle John sang about monks:

Did you ever hear tell of the monks of old?
What a saintly race they were.
They laughed "Ha Ha", and they quaffed "Ha Ha",
And lived on the daintiest cheer.

2

It was very nice living there before the rat came, but sometimes I wished I had someone to play with besides Tibby. If you looked up to the street from the area, you could see many little boys going by. Sometimes they would stop and look down, and some would spit down or throw orange peel at you. I liked to look at the little girls best. Sometimes one would look down and say, 'Hallo, little boy. What's your name?' Some of the little girls carried dolls and I wished that they might drop one down so that I could have it to play with, but they never did. I couldn't get anyone to buy me a doll; they said, 'boys didn't play with dolls — it wasn't proper.'

I thought that the pretty china lady and gentleman which stood on each end of the mantelpiece would do, and asked if I could have them to play with. 'No, you can't. They're Dresden china and cost a lot of money.' But one Sunday morning when they all stayed in bed late, I went down to the breakfast room and climbed up on the high brass fender to look at the pretty lady. Perhaps no one would know if you took her down on the hearthrug and played with her there. Better take the gentleman too, one in each hand, yes. But you couldn't help it if the fender tipped over and you fell down smash in the fireplace.

Then they came running down and said, 'Oh, dear! Oh, dear! Look at that, you bad wicked boy!' but Father said, 'It's no good talking, it's done now, and look at that bump on his forehead.' When they picked up the pieces, the poor lady's head was off and the gentleman had both his nice legs broken and his white fingers chipped off.

It was one morning soon after this that the rat came. They had put a trap in the area because they had seen signs of rats there. So when you went out there one morning and saw a funny-looking animal in a cage and put your finger in to stroke it, your finger got bitten and blood came. Then you went in where they were all having breakfast and said, 'Look'.

For several days after that they talked about the old house

3

and rats and whether they had better move, and about how much money they had got in the bank that Mother had saved from the lodgers' money, and soon after that you had to go to Camberwell and stay with your Uncle John and Aunt Eliza while they moved to a grocers' shop at Peckham.

Then they sent for me but I didn't like the new place much because it had no area where you could look up and see children go by. But dear old Tibby was there, and there were lots of biscuits in the shop.

2

Instead of going downstairs like we did in Duke Street, everything was upstairs at the shop — stairs at the back of the shop went up to a little kitchen and you couldn't play in there much because Mother kept saying, 'For goodness sake, get out of my way,' and if you went down into the shop you got in the way there and got hit with the cane of the long feather brush. Sometimes you fell right down the stairs to the shop and got bumps.

But there was a large front room where you could go and watch the trains going into the station opposite. In the morning soon before the nine o'clock train came in, the Station Master would come out in the station yard and ring a big brass bell and then shout, 'Now for London, gentlemen — now for London.' Then you would see a lot of people come hurrying along with shiny hats and umbrellas and soon after that the train would come in and all would be quiet again.

When you got tired of that, you might go down in the shop and see what Father was doing, and perhaps get a biscuit. So you crept down and watched people coming in to buy things and get money given to them for change.

When the greengrocer man came in from next door to buy some German sausages, Father asked him why the Station Master only shouted out 'Now for London' for the nine o'clock train and not for the others, and the man said, 'Not for Joe. That's the train all the big bugs go on. He's a downy bird and he's making it all right for Christmas.' Then they both laughed, but I kept wondering what train the little bugs went by, and why bugs went at all and who Joe was and what a downy bird was like.

Then when there were no customers in the shop, I went behind the counter where the biscuits were, but I tumbled over a broom and knocked over a lot of tins of salmon. Father got angry and shoved me upstairs and shouted out, 'Can't you keep this damn kid out of the way?' and then Mother answered back and they both got cross and made such a noise that I got frightened and went back to the front room. That's where I found Tibby, who had gone there too to get out of the way.

The next thing they did to keep me out of the way was to send me to Mrs Rudd's school in Asylum Road. Before then I had learned the ABC from wooden blocks and spelt short words by moving the blocks about, so I soon learned to read little tales in one-syllable words out of the school reading books. One of them was about a little boy who was named Tom, same as me. It began, 'Tom fell in the pond. They got him out. He was wet and cold.' There was a lot more about how it served him right because he had been told not to go near ponds. I don't remember whether he died or only caught cold, but I felt sorry for Tom because the only pond I knew was the one on Peckham Rye, and that was all muddy-looking and not a nice pond to fall in.

I liked tales like that one; they made you think and wonder who 'they' were who got him out, and if he could have fallen in without getting wet. There was a nice boy named Harold Warren at the school who lived at the chemist's shop next-door-but-one to us, so we got to be friends and he came in on wet days and played with me in the front room, so after that I was not so sorry that we had left the old house. When we went for walks we put our arms over each other's shoulders and we said that we would always be friends. When the other boys at school got to know that I sometimes brought biscuits from the shop they played with

6

me too, and we had some fine games under the railway arches.

I think Father was sorry we had moved to the new shop. I heard him say that they had paid too much for it and been had, and if things didn't get any better we'd all go in the workhouse. But there were always plenty of biscuits in the shop and tins of salmon and jam and things, so I thought that if we didn't sell them we could live on them for a long time.

Things didn't get any better, so after a time Mother came down and served the customers while Father went out to get orders like he used to when he worked at the tea grocer's in the West End, before we moved. Soon after that the business began to get better and better, and lots more people came to the shop. Sometimes on Saturdays they came in until twelve o'clock at night. Then Father had to get a young man to help them in the shop and take out goods in a basket, and get up orders, and after a while so many orders came in that they bought a pony from Wales and sent the goods out in a cart.

Then they bought another pony and got another young man, but I liked the first one best, Fred Morley. When he came upstairs to tea he always told me lots of funny tales and bits out of the *Arabian Nights*. Sometimes he used to make up tales himself, silly ones, like the one about a boy who came downstairs naked on Christmas morning and went down the garden to pick some apples to make a cake, and how a cat came and barked at him, so he threw one of his boots at it and put one apple in his mouth and two in each pocket and then went indoors whistling. Then Fred would say, 'To be continued in our next,' and eat some more bread and butter. So I couldn't help liking Fred.

As they kept on doing more and more trade at the shop, we had a lot of new clothes and better things to eat, not rice and things out of the shop like we did when we first came. But lots of the customers had things booked and didn't always remember when it was time to pay, and sometimes

7

Father said he didn't know where to turn to get the money to pay his bills. Some customers moved away and didn't pay at all, and then Father said no wonder Peckham was called 'Slopers' Island'.

Two or three of the customers who owed money were schoolmasters who kept small private schools for boys, and one of them said, 'Why not send your boy to my school to work off the debt?' So after a year at the first school, I went to one of them, and then another one, and after that to Mr Bradley's school in Asylum Road. Mr Bradley was the best of them all, and I was glad I went there. He had about thirty pupils and taught us all himself in a large basement room. He took great pains to teach us how to write plainly and draw things. He'd come round behind each of us in turn and show us how to hold the pen and guide our hand. Some afternoons he told us to put away our books, and then he would sit and talk to us. He talked about words and how to pronounce them, and what language many of the words came from; about history and mountains and rivers, the stars and the signs of the zodiac.

I didn't like arithmetic, and neither Mr Bradley nor the other schools troubled to teach me. I expect they knew that I was only to be there a short time to work off the grocery bill, and not a paying scholar like the others.

It was just about this time that a war broke out between Prussia and France. France started it and invaded a small bit of Germany, but the Prussians soon drove them back. Most of the boys were on France's side, and they got me to draw battles on their slates. I always drew lots of Prussians being killed, but soon I had to do it the other way about because the boys liked to be on the winning side.

It was an awful war but only lasted about three months. The French were beaten in a dreadful battle at Sedan, and soon after that Marshal Bazaine surrendered in Metz with over 50,000 soldiers, to half that number of Prussians, without any fighting. Some of the boys said it was good of him because it saved a lot of poor soldiers getting killed, but most of them said he was a worm and that it served him right when he was put on trial and sentenced to death. He did get let off in the finish, and before France could get peace she had to lose Alsace and Lorraine, and promise to pay the Germans two hundred million pounds. We heard that when the Prussians surrounded Paris, the people couldn't get food, so they ate the elephants out of the zoo, and the dogs. Somehow the dogs got to know about it and must have told each other, because many of them in the streets slunk away and hid themselves when a man came along. The boys all felt sorry for the poor animals.

While the war was on, trade at our shop was very good and money came in better, so they began to talk about sending me to boarding school as I was ten years old. One customer whose name was Flint owed rather a big bill for grocery, so he said that his son was at a college in Berkshire and quite as a personal favour he would speak for me to be admitted. 'They only take sons of gentlemen, you know, but leave it to me – my recommendation will overcome any difficulty.'

So the matter was arranged without any trouble, except on my part, but they said, 'It's no good you howling. You've got to go and be educated.'

Then they got me trousers, a best suit, a second-best one, and one for school, and so many of shirts and socks and things, and one morning I was taken down to Berkshire and left at the school.

3

It was pretty miserable that day, and my handkerchief was all wet and dirty. A lady who was there said I had better go and walk around the playground and gardens and get used to the place, because I wouldn't have any lessons to learn that day. I wandered round and into the gardens, and past the gardens I found a farm-yard place with ducks and chickens and a place with pigs in it. Past that was a large field with a lot of cows. I liked looking at the pigs best — they looked so fat and happy. Then a boy came and fetched me in, and I had to wash my hands in a long passage place and then go in to have tea in a big room with long tables.

Mr Flint's son came up to me and said, 'How do you do?' There were a lot of boys there and Flint said, 'This is Lloyd, the new boy, and he's going to be my fag.' The other boys all smiled and said, 'How do you do?' too. They all spoke so nicely and were so well-behaved that I thought it was very nice for me to be at that college with gentlemen's sons.

We had tea with thick slices of bread and butter, but I didn't like the tea much. It wasn't so good as we had at home and there wasn't any jam or things.

Later on when I went up to bed I didn't think I should like it so much. There were nine other boys there in a long room called a dormitory, and after they showed me where my bed was we all undressed. Then they all got round me and pulled my shirt off so that I was all naked and after they had pushed me about and pinched me they picked me up and made me sit on a cold mantelpiece with a po on my head. It came right down to my nose. They said, 'Now you're crowned King of the room and will have to sit on your throne all night.' But soon one of them who was standing near the door said, 'Cavey,' and then they pulled me down and shoved me under the bedclothes, and jumped into bed themselves. A gentleman came in and looked round the room, and after turning out the light said, 'Good night, boys.' They all answered, 'Good night, Sir,' sleepily, so I did too.

It was very quiet in the room then and I was rather tired and glad to go to sleep in such a nice bed, but soon I heard them all getting up again, and one struck a match and lit a bit of candle. Then they came over to me and told me to put on my nightshirt, and asked me if I'd got anything to eat in my box. I wouldn't tell them, because Mother had put a big cake in it for me, but they kept twisting my arms and only laughed when I kicked out at them. Then they turned out all my pockets and found the key and one of them crept out quietly to the passage outside where the boxes were, and he got the cake. When he brought it in they said, 'Corn in Egypt!' and started cutting it up in chunks with a cover of a book. They ate it all up except a small piece they gave me. I couldn't help crying, and there were crumbs in my bed, but somehow I went to sleep.

A loud ringing woke me up in the morning at seven o'clock, and one boy showed me where to go and wash and where the other place was. Then when we'd got dressed, we went across the playground to a big room called the Hall. It had rows of desks and a platform at the end where one of the masters sat. When we'd all got in, the master read out some prayers, and after that the boys did what they said was 'prep', but I didn't do anything — only look about — because I hadn't been examined. At eight the big bell rang again and we all marched two by two to the dining room. I had bread and butter and a cup of warm milk. It was rather thin and bluey-looking and I didn't like drinking it because it made me think of the castor oil I used to have in milk. After break-

11

fast, we went in the playground until nine o'clock, when school commenced.

One teacher took me to a little desk and gave me a book to read out loud. Then he made me write 'knowledge is power' and 'honesty is the best policy', and asked questions about rivers and mountains. I *was* glad he didn't ask me to do any sums. Then he said I was to go in Mr Scudamore's class. I didn't think I should have been put there – they were all bigger boys and lots of the lessons I couldn't do at all. At twelve o'clock we went out in the playground again, and I went round to the farm part and looked at the pigs again. It was a bit smelly there so I moved to the garden and looked at the hollyhocks until the bell went again for us to go in to dinner.

We had to stand while one of the masters said grace in Latin, and then we sat down to dinner. It didn't take long to eat what they gave us. When we went out again, Flint called me aside and gave me some money; he said I was to go out by the little gate in the wall and go down the lane to a little shop with a parlour window. I was to go in there and buy him a tuppenny packet of cocoa and a penn'orth of 'locust beans' and I was to be quick and be sure not to let other boys see me give the things to him, and if I ate any of the locusts he'd skin me.

I went along slowly and kept looking on the ground as if I'd lost something, and when I got to the gate I popped through and went up the lane to find the shop. There was a nice fat lady there and the shop smelled like cabbages and bundles of wood. It was all bunged up with tins of biscuits, bottles of sweets and cakes on plates and heaps of things. I thought I would spend some of the sixpence I had, as I was rather hungry, so I asked the lady if she had any Banbury cakes. She said, 'No, dear, but I've got some nice three-corners,' so I had two of those. They were rather small, but jammy inside. Then I had two more and bottle of ginger beer.

When the lady gave me the things for Flint she said, 'You're a new little boy, aren't you? And where might you have come from?' So I told her Peckham, and she said, 'Well I never! I was in service in Rye Lane when I was a gell — ever been up the Rye?' I said, 'Yes,' and told her about the pond there, and she sighed and said, 'Ah, Sunday night was the time.' Then she kissed me and gave me a large apple. I could hardly get it in my pocket.

When I got back, I found Flint waiting by the gate. He said, 'Where the blazes have you been, you young devil?' Then he counted the locusts and gave me one. I didn't tell him about the apple, but got away from the other boys and went round by the pigs to eat the apple and the locust there.

The boys didn't do anything to me in the dormitory that night, but kept awake telling tales in turn. After a few nights I thought I would tell them some of Fred Morley's silly tales and some out of the *Arabian Nights*. They seemed to like those and it got so that they made me sit up in bed every night and tell them some more. Some nights when I was very sleepy, they would say, 'Wake that kid Lloyd up, somebody,' and Platt minor, who slept next to me, would pull all the clothes off the bed. Once I got so cross that I said a lot of nasty things that I had heard the butcher-man next door to us say to the greengrocer, but they didn't mind a bit and kept teasing me to say more. They had never heard such things as that before, being gentlemen's sons, so I didn't think they knew so much after all. Then I told them a lot of rude words that I had heard London boys say, but they said they knew all *those*.

Next day they must have told other boys in the playground, because they were all running about telling each other to 'go and eat coke', or 'I'll land you one on the conk', as well as 'stow your gaff', and 'go and fry your face'. It got so that it spread all over the school like the measles and the masters spoke about it, but none of the boys told on me.

One evening after tea they asked me to come and see the Common Room. As we went down the long passage, at one part of it they told me to put my hand on the wall and feel

13

how hot it was. They said that a long time ago the school had been on fire and it had never been properly put out, it was still smouldering in the wall, and one day it might break out again and burn us all up. I got very frightened at that, but they said it would be all right if I learned fire drill and if I liked they would teach me. So I said, 'Yes, please,' and they took me into the Common Room and stood me in front of the fire. Then two of them held me so near the fire that my trousers got hot and nearly scorched, and then another boy got behind and pulled my trousers close to my legs. It burnt and hurt so that I hollered like anything, but they kept on doing it and said I would be under-done if they didn't. I found out afterwards that the wall was hot because there was a chimney in there that came up from the big kitchen where they did the cooking.

On Sunday morning we had to march two by two a long way to the church in the town. I didn't know whether I should like it as I had never been to a church before. As we went through the town other boys made faces at us, and some on the other side of the road imitated us marching, and one boy pretended he was dying of laughter. I couldn't help laughing too, but Platt minor said, 'Shut up, you fool. Don't take any notice of them. They're a lot of cads — all the town boys are cads.'

It was a very old church and smelled a bit musty. There were some tombs inside with stone knights lying on top with long spiky shoes, pretty windows of coloured glass with the sun shining through, and one large picture of angels in long nightdresses with large wings on their backs. At the top of the picture there were two fat-faced baby angels with no bodies, only heads, with two little wings coming out behind their ears. We all sat in a lot of seats right down one side of the church, and then a lot of boys marched down the middle. They had long white dresses on and went up by the organ. I saw that some of them were boys out of my dormitory, looking so clean and good.

We had to stand up when the singing started and then sit

14

down again when the preacher began to talk. Then we had to stand up again and say things after him. After that, the preacher didn't want us to stand up again, so I went on looking about. I saw that the headmaster was sitting on the other side of the church where he could see us all. He had a lady sitting with him and next to her was the prettiest and nicest little girl I'd ever seen. She had nice brown eyes and her face was like milk and pink cherries. I kept on looking at her and she was looking across at us too, with her pretty eyes wide open. She kept looking at us as if she was wondering what we were, like a cat does when it looks at the fire. She had such nice brown curly hair, and as the sun shone on it it kept changing colour. Once it looked all bronzy and nice like the crackling on pork, and I thought how nice it would be if that little girl and I were like the fat angels and had no bodies, but had wings on our heads so that we could fly about together. We could put our faces close to each other like they did in the picture, and I kept thinking things like that and got all dreamy, but Platt minor kicked me because we were all standing up again.

As we went along home, I asked Platt minor who that little girl was, and he said her name was Fanny 'Topknot' Tingey. She was a niece of the head's wife and was up from Ely in Cambridgeshire on a visit. I asked him if he didn't think she was very nice, and he said, 'Yes, she's jolly pretty, but girls are no good really. I've got four sisters. Wonder what they'll have the cheek to give us for dinner.'

We did what we liked after dinner. Some went for walks with a teacher, and others went in the Common Room. I went in there too, and some boys were writing letters home to get more pocket-money. One said he was going to 'tap the pater for half a quid and then perhaps he would get five bob.' Others were reading or just messing about, and I asked Platt minor if we were going to church again. He said, 'No, thank the Lord. Only a bit of a pow-wow in Hall this evening.'

I saw that someone had left some crayons on the mantelpiece, so I went up near the fire and got one. I went out to the place they called the bog and drew things on the wall. I could do Mr Gladstone all right there, because his big collar showed up well on the whitewashed wall. Then I went round to see if I could look over into the headmaster's garden. I could hear talking there and a little girl laughing, but the wall was too high, so after listening there a long time I went round and wrote FANNY a lot of times on the wall of the place where the pigs lived.

Soon after that, the weather got fine and warmer, and on one Wednesday we had a holiday and went up the river for a treat. We started after breakfast and walked a long way to the river. There was a big boat like a barge with windows down each side, so the masters and big boys went on top and we small ones went down below. We sat on long seats facing each other with our backs to the windows, so we didn't see much of the scenery. A big horse pulled the boat along, and we had to go through some locks. Once we had to wait a long time while the horse was taken over a bridge so as to pull up from the river bank on that side, so I began to get hungry and hoped we would soon get to the treat. One of the teachers came down with some pieces of cake on a paper. I don't think the boys liked that teacher much because when he offered some of them a bit of cake they said, 'No, thank you,' and because they refused it none of the others would have any. They kept whispering to each other as he came along, 'Stick-jaw muck. Don't take it,' but he kept on offering it right down the line. I thought he was very nice and kind, and when he got to me I said, 'Thank you, sir,' and took a big slice. He said, 'I am glad one boy's got some sense,' and he made me take another lump. After he had gone, all the boys jeered at me and a boy opposite kept pretending to be sick every time I took a bite, but I didn't care. It was a bit puddeny, but nice and sweet. Then Platt minor said I was a dirty sneak and a crawler, but I said I didn't care what I was, not when there was cake, and told him to go and fry his face. The boy opposite said I was a cockney cad, and then I lost my temper and squeezed up what was left of the cake and threw it in his face. He came over and bashed me on the head, and I hit out at him; we both rolled over on to the floor and he kept hitting me on the head. The other boys all got round and said, 'Go to it, ye cripples,' and there was such a row that some of the masters came down and stopped it. I was jolly glad they did, because my head did hurt and his collar had come off in my hand. His ear was bleeding too, but I wasn't so hungry by then.

When the boat stopped, we went to a large field with a tent in it. Inside the tent they gave us a glass of ginger beer and one little meat pie and an orange each, and told us to go in the field to eat them. There was a lot of shoving and pushing, so I couldn't get out easily, and somehow, because I was near the table where the pies were, I got another pie and went out behind the tent. I had a good feed but my head did hurt. Then I went to sleep and didn't wake up until it was time to go home, so I never saw the sports or anything.

They tried to teach me a lot of things at that college and I got to like the lessons, especially dictation and drawing, but I didn't learn much grammar as you can see by what I have written. We had French and Latin and music too, but all I remembered of music was that there were five lines and four spaces. I tried all I could to talk like the other boys did but I didn't see why they should call poorer boys cads just because they didn't dress so well or go to such a good school as we did. I was always glad to go to church on Sundays to look at that little girl, and I tried to make her look at me but she never did. She just gazed at all of us at once, wonderingly-like. I think she must have gone home in a carriage because I never saw her when we went out on our way back from church. I always went round the gardens looking for her, but I never saw her except in church.

After some months, Father and Mother came down one Sunday to see me, and I was allowed to go to the station to meet them. They took me to a hotel where we had a nice dinner, and I was told not to eat so fast. Mother looked at my arms and said that I looked half-starved. Then they gave me *Punch* to look at while they talked. Then we went for a ride in a carriage and had some tea with jam and cakes. When we got back to the station I began to feel miserable again, but Father said, 'Cheer up, Tommy. You're coming home with us.'

So that was the last of that school. I wasn't there long enough to learn much, and all the Latin I remembered was what the other boys had told me about Cave Canem, and Pons Asinorum and Caveat Emptor. I was glad to get home and have enough to eat, but I felt rather sorry that I shouldn't see the pigs or that little Fanny Topknot any more, and I should have liked to have been in that dormitory when a new boy arrived.

4

I wasn't sent to any more schools in Peckham so I had a good time playing with the other boys I knew and going out with Fred Morley in the pony cart when he went for orders. In the evenings when the boys came out of school and had their tea we went up Rye Lane and had games of cricket on the Rye with a shilling bat and a sixpenny hard indiarubber ball. I tried to tell them all about the college I'd been to but they didn't listen much because they wanted to talk too. It was just the same at home. They were too busy to hear about it, but at last they gave me an exercise book and told me to write all about it in that, and to put it all down and not leave anything out. It would be good practice and improve my writing and also get me out of the way. So I did that and I read a lot of Mr Dickens's books that came out in monthly numbers at a shilling each.

On Saturdays they got me to stand outside the shop and watch the cases of eggs which were laid out on the pavement. I used to sell them too. The best were 16 for a shilling, and the cheapest were 24. Now and then I went to stay with Uncle John in Camberwell. He had a large garden and grew all sorts of pretty flowers, but I liked the hollyhocks best of all. You didn't have to stoop down to look at them and they had blooms that kept coming out right up the stem like Excelsior.

The last time I stayed there was when a telegram came to say that our shop had been burnt down in the night and I was to stay where I was for a time. I heard afterwards that our dog had woken them up by barking, and they only just got out in time. It was thought that the fire was caused by cats knocking over packets of matches from the shelves. You see, there were a lot of mice in the shop and the young men used to go out and bring in any stray cat they could find and leave them in the shop all night. I don't know whether the poor cats escaped, but our dog did.

Then Father got a small shop near by and did what trade he could while the burnt shop and house were being put right, but that took a long time and the people at the milk shop started selling all sorts of grocery and then someone opened another grocer's shop round the corner. By the time we went back to our old shop there wasn't much trade left. All the accounts books had been burnt in the fire, so we couldn't prove what customers owed except by what both parties could agree to, or guess at. But many customers didn't guess the same as we did, so some money was lost that way. Some of them wouldn't pay at all.

Then the creditors began to worry Father for their money and he hadn't got near enough to pay them because when he was doing well he never saved any but spent it as fast as it came in. The finish of it was that after struggling on for about a year we were in debt up to our ears. Men came in and took possession, and little tickets saying 'LOT 1' and 'LOT 2' and so on were put on the furniture and things as all had to be sold to pay the creditors so much each. Wages had to be paid too, so Father made out that he hadn't paid Fred Morley any wages for a long time, and that way Fred got a nice bit when he left. I was glad of that. Then it was all up with that shop and everything got upside down and confused, so I was packed off to South Wales to live with my grandmother.

My Granny lived at a large village called Morriston, about three miles from Swansea. She kept a little general shop with goods showing in a parlour window. She seemed to have a little of everything there except bundles of wood.

20

As I was used to shops, I wanted to do all I could to help her. She let me clean the window and dress it up fresh. I made some large signs like shops in Peckham used to have, such as, 'TRY OUR NEW SEASON TEA' and 'WE LEAD. OTHERS FOLLOW'. The customers and the travellers who called did laugh at seeing such tickets in Granny's tiny shop. Then I packed up some sugar in pound cones like they did in London, but the customers didn't like it. They thought they got more sugar when it was wrapped up flat like a sausage roll. I couldn't help her serve customers because most of them spoke Welsh, but by listening and watching I soon knew what most of the words meant and I knew what they said to each other about me, although they didn't think I knew. Although I got to know a lot of the language, I never spoke it because the first time I tried to do so they laughed at me. So I never said a word after that. No one ever paid cash for the goods they bought, but brought the money every fortnight when wages were paid at the mines and works. Granny kept her accounts by making chalk marks on the wall. It was a sort of Welsh short-hand that she had made up herself. There never seemed to be any dispute about the money owing, and when it was paid she rubbed the chalk marks off with her Welsh flannel apron.

There was a large garden at the back, sloping down the hillside. She grew potatoes there and at the bottom was a fat pig in a sty — I was glad to see that and I liked to see it being fed. Granny used to boil pailsful of potatoes and other things mixed with barley meal to feed him. She got most of the stuff out of the shop, and he used to scream blue murder if his breakfast was a bit late. So what with the shop to see to, the gardening, and baking her own bread, you couldn't call Granny lazy.

I had never tasted bread that was so nice as she made — you didn't need any relish for breakfast when you had that. When she made the bread she also made some bake-stone bread like very large muffins. It wasn't done on a stone really, but on a large round thick iron plate that she laid on top of the fire and then put the dough on to cook. When she wanted some bacon for breakfast, she stood on a chair and cut a long slice from the side of bacon that hung on hooks from the ceiling. It was very salty and not smoked like London bacon is. On Sundays we had a special treat for breakfast with bacon. Sometimes it was cockles and other times what they called 'laver bread'. Women came round with the cockles every Saturday from the sea-side, all fresh boiled, and you dried the cockles in a cloth and dipped them in oatmeal. Then you fried them in the bacon fat with the rashers.

The laver bread was a sticky mass of stuff like black dough with tinges of green in it. It was made from sea-weed which women gathered round the Gower coast and then boiled. You cut it in slices and dipped them in oatmeal and fried them, same as you did the cockles. Both those things were very nice, though the look of the 'laver' before it was cooked was enough to put anyone off their feed. They said that laver bread was very nourishing because it had a lot of iodine in it.

Having nice things like that to eat made me think that I should like to live there always, but I often looked across the houses below and right over the valley where the coal mines were, and I watched the Great Western train going all the way to Paddington in London, and wished I was in it going back to Peckham and my friends.

The houses were all built of stone and dotted about in terraces and pairs from the valley right up to the top of the hill, with unpaved roads and steep stony paths between. I used to walk around and wonder why they built such fine large stone chapels and yet left the path and road outside the building just as it was before, all rough and muddy. It's like spoiling the ship for a ha'p'orth of tar. You could look right into the colliers' cottages as you went by. The front doors were left open and you could see a row of a dozen brass candlesticks on the mantel, and on the wall over that a lot of other brass and tin things hanging up, all

22

bright and highly polished. Many of them had a mahogany chest of drawers in the living room polished up so that the firelight showed in it like a mirror. The floors were of red brick and covered with yellow sand. Many men got a living by bringing round sand every week in barrows. These cottages reminded me of some poetry I had once heard recited. It was about little Jim, a collier's only child, who wasn't expected to live. It began,

> The cottage was a thatched one,
> The outside old and mean,
> Yet everything within that cot
> Was wondrous neat and clean.

But the cottages in Morriston were roofed with thick Welsh slates. Also there didn't seem to be any only children. They had a lot in most of the houses. You'd see a baby being nursed in a shawl and one or two other little ones looking out over the doorboard, and women would walk along with a baby tucked in their shawls while they carried a basket of goods on their heads and knitted stockings as they went down the stony hillside. I expect they went in for babies about there more than where little Jim lived. Lots of the cottages were whitewashed all over. On fine mornings the lady of the house would come out with a pail and a long-handled brush and do over the front of the house. Some mixed colour with the limewash, yellow or red mostly, and when they were done they looked very bright and clean, but the colours didn't always go together well. Sometimes you'd see a cottage done in yellow between two others done in different shades of red.

But the brightness soon faded because of the coal dust on the roads and the smoky fumes from the furnaces of the copper and tin works. Then out she'd come again with her whitewash brush — those Welsh women were always fighting the dirt, but it was a one-sided battle.

Most of the children, especially the boys, were only really

23

clean on Saturday night and part of Sunday. Their hands and faces were clean every morning but the dust and fumes made everything they'd touch outdoors grimy, so the boys quickly got dirty again and the parents gave it up as a bad job.

There was a fine view from the back door of Granny's house. You could look right over the roofs of the houses below at night and see the bright lights of the steel and spelter works' blast furnaces and the flames pouring out of the tops of great chimneys. The lights kept changing from white to red and then violet. It was better than fireworks — they didn't go out just as they began to look pretty like fireworks do.

Granny had a lot of books, very old and worn. One was *Foxe's Book of Martyrs* with all the esses printed like effs and many pictures of poor men and women being tortured or burnt. There was a large old book of *Pilgrim's Progress* too, so I had plenty to read when I couldn't get anything else, but those two books always made me feel miserable. Granny gave me a penny a week to buy the *Young Folks Budget*. It came out every Thursday. There was a fine tale in it by Mr Stevenson, called 'The Sea Cook'. I heard afterwards that it was made into a book and then they called it *Treasure Island*. I got it at a shop at the top of Morriston where they sold bottles of ink and tobacco and papers. I used to go up there two or three times on Thursday to see if that paper had come in from London. Sometimes it wouldn't come until Friday and I went about miserable and wished I was back in London so as to get it sooner.

We had a tallow candle to read by at night but the big fire helped to make the room light. Some evenings Granny would tell me long tales from Welsh history and things she remembered. One was about the Rebecca riots when she was young. She said that a lot of men, farmers' sons and others, used to go about at night with their faces blacked and led by a big man on a horse. He was dressed in women's things and was called Rebecca. Well, they went about breaking down and burning tollgates and sometimes if they didn't like the tollhouse keeper they took his furniture out and burned that too. She said that the big landowners used to own the roads and lanes so that they put up gates and charged everyone who went through with a cart or wagon. Sometimes you had to pay four tolls before you could get your goods to market.

Another fine tale was about a dog called Gelert. Ever so many years ago there was a Welsh chief who had a little baby and he seemed to have carted the baby everywhere with him, so perhaps its poor mother was dead. One day he went away hunting or something, so he left the baby in bed and told his big dog Gelert to take care of it. Well, when he got back he saw that the baby had disappeared — the bedclothes were all tumbled about and bloody and the dog had blood all over his jaws. So he thought at once that Gelert had eaten his baby. He called it Hell-hound and killed it with his sword. Then just after he had done that a little cry came from the bed and he found his baby quite safe under the tumbled bedclothes, and just under the bed was a great dead wolf with its throat all torn. Then the Chief was stricken with grief at what he had done to his faithful hound and he had it buried in a hero's grave and put up a big stone in its memory. You can see its grave now if you go to Wales. It is called Bedd-Gelert.

That story made me cry, and I thought what a wonderful old lady Granny was to remember things like that and tell about them so well, and yet she couldn't write or read much. When she was young, she said, she lived at a farm in Carmarthen and was much better off. When she got married she rode home from church on a horse sitting behind her husband, and when they got to their new home he lifted her up and carried her over the doorstep. She said that was the proper thing to do in Wales when you got married. Then she told me that one of her ancestors was a friend of a king, and he had taken a band of his farm men to help his friend Henry Tudor to fight against King Richard the Third, and after the victory he was knighted on Bosworth Field. I thought how fine it would have been to have told those tales to the boys at that college — those and 'The Sea Cook'.

I was left to mind the house on Sunday evenings when Granny went to chapel. I wasn't taken because they thought I wouldn't understand the Welsh service. I had several aunts and cousins living near and they used to call in each other's houses and collect a party and then go in a band to chapel. So I had to fetch out the *Martyrs* and *Pilgrim's Progress* again, but I soon got the hump over those. I wouldn't have dared to tell anyone, but privately I thought 'Christian' was rather a cad to think so much of his own safety that he went away on tramp leaving his wife and little children to get on as best they could. And Bunyan needn't have sneered so much at the 'man with the muck rake'. Helping to cultivate the ground was better than going about star-gazing.

One Sunday night I thought I would try to make the grandfather clock go. It was a very old one and would only tick a few times and then stop. Everybody used to laugh about it because it was always tea time by it. I thought that perhaps the weight inside the case wasn't heavy enough, so I tied a flat iron on as well. Then the clock went for nearly five minutes before it stopped. So I tied another iron on with one of my bootlaces, and then it kept on going all right. I was proud then; I turned the hands round until it showed half past seven. I wouldn't say anything, but wait and see if they noticed it. Then they would say how clever I was.

It was quarter past eight when Granny returned and three aunts came in with her, just to sit down and have a talk before they went home. The tea things were brought out and after they had a cup of tea they started talking about the people they had seen in chapel and what they had on. Then Granny cut me a slice of bread and butter and told me to go to bed. She looked at the loaf then and saw there was a big hole in the centre of it. She dropped the knife and said, 'Dear me, a coffin it is.' She went all white and trembly and the others looked frightened too. Then they spoke about the people they knew who were ill and wondered which one was going to die. One aunt said she had seen a 'corpse candle'

26

floating over the surface of the canal on Saturday night — that was a sure sign. And another remembered about the three crows that perched on the roof of the Lamb and Flag the day before Williams, the landlord, hung himself. I didn't like that talk, it made me feel all creepy. but I didn't go to bed. I stood at the bottom of the stairs listening. They sat closer together and looked over their shoulders to the dark part of the room and sat thinking. Then Aunt Edith remembered about the big black dog that had crossed the path of Sheeni-Shopbutcher the night before her third husband died and when she put her hand down to stroke it, it wasn't there. It was a ghost of a dog come to give warning.

Then when they were quiet and thinking of more things like that to say, the chain in the clock broke and the weight and things fell down to the bottom of the clock-case and made a noise like a gun going off. They all jumped up and screamed and chairs fell over. The people next door came running in, and one of the aunts was laughing and crying at the same time and kicking up her feet. They made such a row that I thought I'd better go up to bed while I was safe and not say anything about making the clock go.

Soon after that, the school inspector found out that I was under-age and sent me back to school again, so I was sent to the large national school near by. All the boys had to take fourpence a week. If they forgot on Monday morning they were told to bring it in the afternoon, and if they didn't they got the cane. There was a pretty rough lot of boys at that school and they didn't like me much. When they were in the playground all they seemed to enjoy was knocking each other about and fighting. I never saw boys fight so much. A boy would come up to me and say, 'I'll fight you,' and if I didn't want to he'd fetch his little brother and say, 'Go on Shoni — hit him. I'll see he doesn't hurt you.' I reckoned that they were a lot of cads but I didn't let them hear me say so. But after a time they let me alone because my cousin Jack could fight and beat any of them and they were afraid he would interfere. Once after school he told two small boys that he would fight 'em both at once on his knees with one hand behind him. So a whole crowd of them went to a field and those boys had their big brothers with them. Jack went on his knees and kept both those boys at bay. They didn't hit him much, and then when he reached out and gave them one or two nasty ones the brothers started on Jack and got behind and kicked him. So that made me cross and I hit out at them all anyhow and Jack got up and punched them all over the place. They all ran away then. Dirty cads.

There were four classes in that school and each teacher had about fifty boys to look after. They hadn't much time to show any boy how to set about doing the problems in arithmetic, so I went on my happy way and never did any right. I didn't know how to do them and had many 'handers' for not doing homework sums. I used to put down any figures that looked right and chance it. If I'd had someone like dear old Mr Bradley to give me a hint I might have done as well as the others.

The only lesson in Natural History we had was about the cuckoo, and it was a song that the boys had to sing when they had singing practice. It was sung to the tune of 'The Ash Grove', and I had never heard boys sing so well as they did without music. Perhaps you would like to know the words of that song, which tells you so much about the cuckoo.

> The cuckoo she's a fine bird, she sings and she flies,
> She brings us good tidings and tells us no lies.
> She sucks the sweet flowers, for to make her voice
>   clear,
> And when she cries 'Cuckoo' the summer is near.

I got a hander for not singing with the others so after that I kept watch and opened my mouth and threw back my head like gargling, the same as the other boys did.

Once my home lessons had a problem about how much water there would be in a cistern, so after struggling with it for over ten minutes I put down some figures that were so much out of reason that the teacher said I had done it on purpose — perhaps I had. Anyhow, the headmaster caned me so much that my hand swelled up and there was a weal like a piece of rope right across it. I couldn't do anything that morning except twist about in pain and think of the beastly things I would do to that master when I grew up. He wasn't a very big man and in a few years' time I'd be strong enough to jump on him and grind his face in the mud.

But in a week's time he marched all my class into a classroom where we sat in a sort of gallery while he stood up at a desk and read to us about William Tell, and on other days he read bits from *Robinson Crusoe* and all of *Sinbad the Sailor*. We sat as quiet as mice and enjoyed those readings, so I thought he wasn't such a bad chap after all, and I forgot about the things I was going to do to him. I am glad now that I did — I might have got hung.

Once when we had a General Knowledge lesson, I was the only one who knew what verdigris was, and was sent up to the top of the class for the first and only time. Another thing that was easy for me was the dictation lesson. Once when I had finished long before the others I drew some pictures of pigs and Mr Gladstone on my slate and the teacher saw me doing it. He took my slate up to the headmaster, and I was told to stay in after school so I knew that I was going to cop it again. But when the boys had all gone, the master asked me a lot of questions about the schools I had been to before and other things, but he didn't punish me. Soon after that, the teacher told me one afternoon to go in a small side room and hear some small boys do their reading. I was to read a small piece out of a history book first and they were to read it after me in turns. It wasn't very successful — those boys kept laughing and mocking me because of the London way I talked. It was so different from the way the Welsh boys spoke English. So I wasn't much better as a teacher than I was as a scholar.

Some evenings after school my cousin Jack tried to teach

me how to fight better. He did it in his back garden and knocked me about a good bit. He said that when you were fighting a boy it was best to get him so that he'd have his back against a wall. Then when you hit him hard on the head he would fall back on the wall and get another knock from that, but when I tried to do it the boy dodged and I hurt my knuckles. I did learn a good way to hit 'em under the jaw near the ear, though.

Well, that's about all I can tell you about that school. It was the last I went to and I might have learnt more there if the teachers hadn't had so many boys in each class. Why I left was because Father had come to Swansea. He had a job as Commission Agent for a London firm, so I had to go and live with them.

As I had never been to a sea-side place I thought Swansea was splendid. It had miles of lovely sands round the Bay and on clear days you could see right over to the Devon coast. If you climbed up the big hill at the back of the town you had a fine view of the docks and the Mumbles light-house. You could see the tug boats going out and bringing in the sailing ships with their sails rolled up. Then the tugs would bring others out of the harbour and when they'd got them a good way out in the Bay the ships would put their sails up and away they went, making a very pretty sight.

The school inspector never troubled about me and I was let to run about the town and do just what I liked, but most times I went on the sands. I hadn't had any new clothes since I left Peckham so it didn't matter much if I did knock them about a bit. I soon found boys to play with and when they had their holidays from school we used to run about naked on the sands all day. There were a lot of bathing machines up where most of the people went, but about a quarter of a mile on a deserted part towards the Mumbles there was a red mark down the sea-wall, and you were allowed to bathe there with nothing on. On hot days we brought bread and butter and a bottle of water and were naked savages all day. When the tide came in we bathed, and I soon learned to swim, and after that we laid about on the warm sand and then ran races and played games all day until the tide came in again, and then we had another swim. Some days we were too lazy to go as far as the red mark, but undressed where we oughtn't to. Then the bathing machine man would tell a policeman and we got chased. Once we had to run away naked right over the public road into a field on the other side, dropping a boot or socks and things as we went. The policeman never caught us and I don't think he really wanted to. Perhaps he'd done the same when he was a boy.

Some days when the tide was a long way out we went ever so far to the rocks and stones that were left uncovered and we filled our caps with winkles that we found there. Once a whole lot of cockles must have come in from the Gower coast. They would bury themselves in the ridges of sand left by the receding tide. When it got known, hundreds of boys came and gathered them in and then the cockles must have thought that Swansea wasn't a nice place to emigrate to, because we never found any more there.

Then the winter came and it brought with it some bad luck for us. Father lost his job as agent, and as he never saved any money when he'd got the chance, things got a bit awkward. His idea about money was to spend it as fast as it came in. He earned quite good wages while he stuck to work, but he got tired of it rather soon and wanted a rest or a change. Still, after a long rest, he generally managed to get another engagement because he always dressed well and looked so smart. He used to say that a good appearance was everything, and if you'd got cheek as well you could go anywhere and do anything. He said that most people were fools and took people at their own valuation, and when you were a commercial traveller some small shopkeepers felt it an honour to be able to give an order to such a well-dressed gentleman.

But during the resting time we were sometimes very hard up and I didn't always get enough to eat. Once I had to go and get a small supply of coals in a carpet-bag, and another time get some tea, sugar, milk and bread and yet bring back change out of sixpence. Some days I went for a long tramp past the Mumbles and got a big lot of winkles, mussels and cockles as well as limpets. The limpets were harder to get. You had to snatch them off the rocks quickly before they got aware of you. If you touched them tenderly, they stuck so tight to the rocks that you couldn't get them off without smashing them. That lot of shell fish made a good meal and Mother called it a mixed grill.

Another thing, if you went along the beach as the tide was coming in, a good lot of pieces of wood and bits of coal could be collected, but it was a long job and a cold one on a winter morning. Then I managed to get a lot of bits of waste wood from some men who were building a row of houses near us. I hung around there a good deal and watched them working and then got friendly with them, so they let me take bits of wood that were lying about, and they got me to fetch beer for them. After a while, they let me make a fire of shavings and wood, and hot up their cans of tea. I'd go errands just before the one o'clock gun went off and buy sausages, corned beef and cheese and also some more beer. While they were having dinner, I searched round and got some larger chunks of wood and put them handy so that I could collect them in the evening when the men had gone. They each gave me a penny on Friday, so that was something else to take home.

Although we were very poor at times, Father would never pawn his clothes. His watch and chain and ring would go but his clothes, he said, was the armour wherein he trusted.

Then suddenly the clouds would roll by and things would look bright again for a time. While we lived in Swansea, we seldom stayed in a house for much more than three months, because there was nearly always some unpleasantness with the landlord. Houses were quite easy to get with many standing empty for a long time, and landlords were quite glad to let a house to a respectable well dressed tenant who readily agreed to pay all rates and taxes. I never remember any rates being paid but perhaps the accounts hadn't come in before we moved, or if they had they were overlooked in the hurry of moving.

33

One terrace house we lived in had a large shed at the end of the garden. The back gate opened on to a narrow lane which served as a back entrance to our row and the houses that backed on to us. While we were there Father had an agency to sell a new kind of disinfectant that had just been invented. The firm's main factory was in London. When you put a little of this stuff in water, it turned white like milk. He got lots of orders for this and drew plenty of commission, but when repeat orders were sought it was another matter. The shopkeepers were 'bunged up with the blooming stuff'. He had to look about for some other way of making a bit, so he went in for dealing in small and cheap lots of things bought at auction sales — cleaning them up and re-selling them at a good profit. Brass and iron bedsteads, magic lanterns, models of ships, cases of stuffed birds and similar things all found new homes after an advertisement had been put in the local paper. I was kept busy with black enamel, paraffin and brick-dust, making the things look new.

The most interesting lot he bought was four little pigs. We got those at bargain price at the cattle market auction, and two little drover boys steered them into our garden shed. The bye-laws said that people mustn't keep pigs in the town, but father said that what you mustn't do and what you did do were two different things. So we started keeping pigs for profit. I was given the job of attending to them. They said, 'Tom likes pigs,' but I should have had to do it anyway. A corn merchant obliged by supplying some sacks of barley meal, and we paid for a sack of sawdust to put on the floor of the shed.

So I did what I'd seen Granny do and boiled pailsful of meal and things, potato peelings and waste vegetable stuff that I picked up in the market. It all went in, and those little things did enjoy it. What with feeding them, sweeping out the shed and laying fresh sawdust, I was kept pretty busy, but I found time to watch them dining and then see them snuggle up together and go to sleep. I got quite fond of them after a few days and I think they liked me, because they were always pleased to see me come in. A good way to make pigs like you is to scratch their backs with a hard broom; they can stand any amount of that. I gave each of them a name, three of them I called after boys at that college and the other one I called Fanny.

I had to wear a very old pair of trousers when I was pig-man, and change into another pair afterwards, but after a time I got tired of doing so and kept the piggy pair on all day and other boys didn't play with me so much as before. The way those pigs grew up and fattened was surprising. They got so strong that they nearly knocked me over when they rushed up for the food I took in. Keeping the shed clean got harder and there was a great heap of sweepings outside, so on the quiet I did some 'commercial travelling' and got orders from neighbours who did gardening, and I charged a penny for two big pailsful delivered free. I didn't tell anyone but kept that money. Some I saved and the rest bought the *Boys of England*. I was always served quickly at the paper shop when I went in with my piggy trousers on.

What I've got to tell you now is a bit sad and I expect you'll be sorry too. One morning when I'd used up the last of the barley meal in making breakfast for them, I found the shed door open and the pigs gone. It seems that a quarter's rent was four weeks overdue and the landlord, having got wind that we were keeping pigs — as anyone might have done if they went by our shed — had sent a bailiff who put his hand over and unbolted the gate. Then he carted my little friends away. I did feel sad and sorry and a bit wild too, after doing all that work for nothing, but I couldn't help it, so I made a bonfire and burnt my old trousers, and if that land-lord had been there I'd have shoved him on the fire too.

By listening to talk that went on at home about pigs and landlords, I learned a lot about the law: a bailiff mustn't force an entry to a house, but can only come in if a door is opened for him or if he finds it open, and he must do it before sunset and not at all on Sundays or Good Friday. If he does you can push him out. If the doors are never opened, and a tenant goes in and out of his house through a window, then the bailiff can go in through the window too, but he mustn't break his way in. This makes it awkward for a landlord if no one answers the door. I expect that's what happened before the pigs went. I heard a lot about what that landlord deserved to have done to him and different ways to have revenge and get level with him, but nothing came of it. It was too much trouble, so they finished up by saying that 'Providence pays debts without money', and left it at that. Just the same, we put a strong padlock on the garden gate and didn't leave anything in the shed.

After that I had the job of cleaning up and black-enamelling old iron bedsteads and things bought at sales. There were also a lot of parrot cages got very cheaply at an ironmonger's shop where the proprietor had gone bankrupt. They were very tarnished and a bit rusty but I made them look all right with paraffin and brick-dust.

Just about this time there was a big war between Russia and Turkey and nearly everybody was talking about the Siege of Plevna where Osman Pasha was holding that city against hordes of Russians, and they all admired his bravery. Every now and then he'd make a sortie and dash out doing a lot of damage and worrying the Russians no end, and then get back to Plevna and keep the enemy at bay again. It was months before they had to surrender and then it was only through lack of food. I expect you will wonder why I am telling you about this, but if you wait a bit you will see why.

A few days after the next quarter's rent was due, that landlord started being unpleasant again. He must have been a hasty, nasty-tempered and lawless sort of man. Law or no law he didn't care what he did. One morning, when Mother was away helping a lady friend with spring cleaning, he came with a bailiff and other men before dinner and started breaking in our back gate. When we saw what he was doing, we bolted and barred our back door and made it stronger by fixing the long side-irons of bedsteads against it, one end under the lock and another fixed under the top bolt. The irons reached across the kitchen and were wedged into the front of the dresser, so he wouldn't be able to open that door in a hurry.

By the time this was done in the house, the garden gate had been broken down and the invaders came up and banged at the door. They tried to force it open by banging themselves against it. Then they had a go at the back room window and broke a pane of glass so as to put their hands in and undo the catch, but father used a poker when they put their fingers on the catch and they gave up. Then they had another go at the back door with a crowbar, but although they wedged it in and broke the lock and bolts, they couldn't get it open.

While they were doing this, the irons kept shifting from the shock and it was my job to keep fixing them back. I was very frightened and trembling, but I managed somehow. When they couldn't break open the back door, one man took a run and banged himself against it, and then the landlord took the crowbar and banged right and left making splinters fly, but nothing happened.

During this time, a lot of people gathered in the back lane. Neighbours looked out of bedroom windows and over garden walls and children on their way from school came right in our garden. Word must have gone round that a bit of sport was on, because before the siege ended there was a big crowd of sightseers, mostly men, who seemed to have nothing to do just then. People climbed up and stood on the garden walls and lots of women must have left off getting dinner for their old man; they stood on chairs in their gardens or in neighbours' gardens nearest the show. It was a working-class neighbourhood and the people there didn't like landlords and hated bailiffs, so they were all on our side, and each time the landlord failed to break the door they set up a chorus of jeers and laughter. Each of the men tried with the crowbar and one got angry with the landlord and told him to do it himself. 'If I can't shift it, nobody can — I don't know what they've got against the B—— door.' One of the irons got dislodged and fell on my wrist and hurt like anything, and after that I wasn't frightened any more, and it's a good job they didn't break in just then, because I would have jabbed one of the irons in their faces. Father was rushing about with his red beard bristling; I think he was as excited as I was. Then they left off for a bit and had a talk together while the crowd kept laughing and jeering. The bailiff said, 'Borrow a ladder from somewhere,' So one man went off and then there was a long interval. The crowd waited too and exchanged remarks, and I went and had some bread and cheese. Other people came until the land at the back was quite full. Husbands who had come home to dinner joined their wives in the gardens. Someone started singing, 'Wait till the clouds roll by, Jenny,' and they all joined in and laughed.

When the man came with the ladder he could hardly get through the crowd. He put the ladder up to the back bedroom window and I was told to see about it, so I took a broom and went up. When I got there, a man had just got the window open so I pushed the broom at his face, but he dodged back in time. Then I used the broom to push the ladder away. It went nearly perpendicular and the man started to scramble down, falling off when he was half-way down. The crowd scattered and the ladder fell on the place where the pig sweepings used to go. All the people round cheered like anything, and I leaned out of the window and waved the broom. The landlord went ramping mad. He told one of the men to go and ask Dawson to bring his sledge-hammer.

So there was another pause and I went down to look after the kitchen door again. When Mr Dawson started work on that door with his sledge-hammer, I soon found that it wouldn't do to stand too close, for in about two minutes he had the door all smashed to flinders and one of the bedstead irons broke in the front of the dresser. I went and sat on the stairs while they all came in, and then a proper row started. Several men neighbours came in too and said that they were quite ready to chuck the lot out. 'Only say the

38

word, Mr Lloyd.' Then the bailiff announced that he had come to take possession unless the quarter's rent was paid together with his fee, and to his astonishment the money was at once handed over. As it happened, we had a bit of money in hand just then. Father said, 'Here's your money, and please understand that legal action will be taken against all concerned.' The landlord used a lot of bad language, so he was told that unless he and his crew were out of the house in three minutes they would be ejected 'without undue violence'. The neighbours said, 'Hear, hear. That's the talk — we'll show him.'

After the landlord left, they fetched cans of beer from the Public at the corner and spent the rest of the afternoon talking and laughing over what had happened. They said it was the best bit of sport they had seen for a long time and as good as the Turks at Plevna. There were about ten of the neighbours there who didn't seem to have any work to go to, or if they had they didn't trouble about it. It was all very pleasant and jolly. They sent for more beer and I had some of it. I was rather sorry that Mother had missed all the fun.

After everybody had gone, we nailed up pieces of wood from the broken door across the garden gate, and made that secure, and then pasted paper over the broken window. We couldn't do anything to the place where the kitchen door had been, so we left it and if the rain came in, it did. It would rot the floorboards and serve that landlord right — bashing our house about like that.

A night or two after, when they were talking about it at 'The Rising Sun' where they used to meet to talk about business, one of them who was a solicitor said, 'If you leave it to me, Mr Lloyd, I'll put him through it.' So he wrote to the landlord and said he was instructed to commence an action for damages for illegal distraint, and that no more rent would be paid until the damage done to his tenant's house was made good. This must have frightened the landlord because his solicitor called and asked us to settle the matter without going to court. So that was agreed to, and after our solicitor had got his whack we had quite a good sum of money, enough to carry on with for a long time, and I had a new suit of clothes out of it. I had wanted one for a long time. I couldn't help thinking how funny it was the way things turn out, so that we got level with him for taking my pigs, and I wondered whether it was right that 'Providence pays debts without money'.

Our next job was to try to sell those parrot cages, and we began to think we never should. Nobody seemed to have a pet parrot without a cage, but we got to know that a bird could be bought cheap at the sailors home near the docks. We were lucky to get several there, so we advertised 'Parrot and Cage for Sale'. When we had replies I had to take the bird in its cage for the buyers' approval. I was given a lot of instructions about what to say if the people asked many questions, but I forgot most of it and did the best I could to sell the things, and I did have a job to answer all the questions. They all wanted to know if the parrots could talk, and I said, 'Yes', because I had been told that all parrots *can* talk but some were slow in learning or nervous in a strange place. I always said that the bird didn't swear, which was quite true. This seemed to satisfy them and we sold several at a very good profit.

I think some of the old ladies bought them because of the nice shiny cage as much as anything; the birds didn't look very happy. They had pretty green feathers but there was a nasty look in their eyes as if they wanted to take it out of somebody, and I felt a bit sorry for some of those ladies.

We got up a raffle for some cages of stuffed birds that we hadn't been able to sell, but the iron bedsteads had got knocked about and parts were broken, so those had to go as 'old iron'. When all the things were clear we moved from that house, and this time they said that they wouldn't have any more to do with landlords of houses, but take apartments somewhere. We went to quite a nice apartment with steps up, and we paid the rent every week to a Mr Davies who had the rest of the house.

It was a bit noisy at the back because there was a large field where boys came to play in the evening, but I liked it because our back fence was broken down and I could get in the field quickly when I wanted a game.

Soon after this, I was told that as I was thirteen I had better look for some sort of employment instead of loafing about and wearing out boots. I answered an advertisement and got engaged as office boy at a brewery. I had to start at nine in the morning until six at night, and I was to have five shillings a week. They said I wasn't to be afraid of work because 'they worked like niggers there', and I said, 'Yes, sir. I'm used to work.' But I didn't think much of what niggers did, because the work I had to do was quite easy and I had a lot of spare time. I had to light the office fire, take orders and messages up the yard to the brewery men, address envelopes and copy letters in a big press. On two days each week I had to go with the traveller when he drove out into the country to get orders. I had to stay in the trap and mind the horse while he was in the inns, and many times I had to wait an awful time before he came out. I used to take something with me for dinner and some days the lady who kept the inn would bring me out a cup of home-brewed beer. All the inns brewed beer, but bought barrels of our stronger ale for their richer customers.

On Thursdays I had to ladle out and sell yeast, which they called barm. Women who made their own bread came for it, or sent their children mostly for twopenn'orth's in their own jugs. Quite a lot would come in, and I was kept busy. It was a messy job, so I had to take off my jacket and tie a sack apron round me. I generally sold about ten shillings' worth, and then I had to wash and go back to the office.

Once when I was thirsty, I asked the brewer for a drink of water. He was quite horrified and said, 'Don't drink that bloody stuff! Have some of this,' and then he drew me a small can of beer from a big barrel. He was a fat kind-looking man and I thanked him very much. There seemed rather a lot in the can, but I managed to drink it — it *was* nice and cool.

41

But it was very different from 'home brew' and when I got back to the office I felt rather silly and wanted to laugh at nothing. I couldn't hold the pen properly and made an awful mess on the envelopes. When I wrote names of towns like 'Ystalyfera' or 'Llangyfelach' the words looked funnier than they usually did. The clerk noticed it and I had to tell him about the beer. Then he told me that I wasn't to let the brewer give me any more beer. After that I used to go and draw a little drop for myself when there was no one about, but not nearly so much as that first can.

In spare time I looked in at every part of the brewery and got friendly with the men. I liked best to see the cooper making barrels to hold 36 gallons, and also tiny ones called pins that held 4½ gallons. The men were always ready to talk and tell you about their trade if you listened with patience.

It was interesting, too, to go in the malt house and see them turn barley into malt. They shovelled the barley into great shallow troughs and then sprinkled it with water, and in a day or so tiny green shoots began to grow out of the grain. If you lay down on your side and looked along the trough that way, it looked like a level field of light green grass. They didn't let it grow much, but shovelled it into a kiln that had a fire beneath it. Then the little shoots turned brown and dropped off, and the barley which had swelled up became crisp and tasted sweet. When this was done it was called malt and was ready to be boiled up to make beer. The little shoots that dropped off were wasted, but they were nice to put in your pocket and chew instead of sweets, except that there was such a lot that you soon got sick of them.

The owner of the brewery was a proper chemist and he was very busy on brewing days. He got me to help him with his gauging instruments and thermometers. I had to enter figures in a book as he called them out, and afterwards clean and pack the things away. Once he asked me if I'd like to be a brewer, and said that if I did I'd have to learn mathematics and study to be a chemist. I didn't tell him so, but I couldn't see much hope for me to do that — not on five shillings a week.

Another thing I did was to look through the books when I was left alone in the office, and I found that none of the men got more than twenty-five shillings a week, and the clerk who kept the books and did all the invoices only got a pound, and he was a grown-up young man. I also saw that the office boy before me had been paid six shillings a week and the money he had taken for barm wasn't nearly as much as I took in. I didn't say anything about it but I began to think that brewing wasn't much of a trade.

At this time, there were a lot of teetotallers about. There was a regular wave of teetotallism all over Wales just then, and children in Sunday schools were got to sign a solemn pledge not to drink intoxicating things as long as they lived. It was a good job I didn't go to Sunday school, or they might have got me to sign too! I shouldn't have liked to make a promise like that and then break it and go to hell. Thousands of children did sign and grown-ups as well, and one day when there was a temperance fete in our town the procession seemed endless. First came hundreds of little girls with white dresses and pretty sashes, then lots of boys in their best, with clean faces and all wearing little blue ribbons. They all looked proud of themselves and good. The banners they carried said they were 'The Good Templars'. Following them there was a band, and after that a procession of grown-up people. Most of them looked pale and hungry. Their banner said 'Sons of the Phoenix', and then came another lot with a banner saying that they were 'Rechabites', but they looked like ordinary people to me. The procession took half an hour to go by and the brewery people came out and watched it and made rude remarks.

After it was all over, I thought and thought about it, and it seemed to me certain that when those children grew up beer wouldn't be wanted any more, so perhaps it would be better to look out for a job in some other trade.

Mr Frietag was a pawnbroker in Down Street. It was quite a small shop and now and again he put a notice in his window, 'Respectable Lad Wanted Good Writer'. Boys didn't seem to stop with him long, but perhaps they weren't so good as I was, so I thought I would have a try for the job. If I got more than five shillings a week I would get more pocket-money — I was only getting tuppence a week for my papers. I thought at first that I wouldn't say anything at home about extra money, but keep it for myself, but afterwards I realized that it might be found out, so perhaps it was best to be honest. One evening I went and saw Mr Frietag, and after some talk he said he would engage me and offered me four shillings a week. I said I wanted seven, please, and he cried, 'Mein Gott. Goot efening.' But as I was going out he called me back and started telling me how easy the work was. All I'd have to do was to write out the pawn-tickets and enter the loans in a book. He mentioned that he didn't open on Saturdays because it was his Sabbath, so 'it vos only a fif-day veek', and I could get some other job on Saturday and make money that way too. I told him that I had been to a boys' college and learned mathematics and Latin, but he smiled and said he didn't want those things in his trade, only how to reckon up 25 per cent. Then he said he'd make it five shillings but I'd have to be honest. He'd just got rid of a boy named Villiam who was a 'goot boy for vork, but vas a tief'. I told him about the barm that I was trusted to sell at the brewery, so he thought for a bit and looked as if he was going to cry. At last he said he would give me six shillings a week and I could start next week, so I said, 'Yes, sir. Thank you.' When I gave notice at the brewery, they offered me another shilling a week to stay on, but it was too late then. The clerk wrote out a reference for me saying I was honest and all that.

The work at Mr Frietag's was easy to learn, but the hours were much longer. For one thing, he couldn't write English. Perhaps if he had he wouldn't have employed a boy at all, not but what he found plenty for me to do besides the tickets.

We were very busy taking in pledges on Monday mornings, and the parcels had to be pulled up in a kind of lift to the room above, where they were stacked on shelves right round the walls. On Friday nights lots of the things would be taken out again and I had to go up and search for the numbered parcels. It took a long time to find some of them and he kept shouting, 'Be qvick — vot a time — vot a time.'

Most of the parcels contained men's Sunday suits, but there were many other things as well. Sheets and boots and children's clothes were taken in, and on Monday most of the things would come back again. Now and again, on quiet days, I had to go up and search for parcels that had been left there for more than a year. We used to brush the things up and put them in the window for sale. If we sold it for more than we'd lent on it, I had to enter the sale in a book in case the person who pawned it came and enquired. If they did, we had to pay the pawner the balance less interest. But nobody called and enquired while I was there.

Another job was to polish up the watches and jewellery in the window. Some of the watches were very good ones and were priced quite cheap, and I wished I could afford to buy one. I'd always wanted a watch. There were a lot of wedding rings on sale too. Mr Frietag said that 'vimmen' didn't redeem them unless they were young and hadn't been married long; the old ones bought a cheap brass ring to wear and the old man never noticed. Most of the women who brought things on Monday morning were pretty fat and looked as if they liked beer. Sometimes they and Mr Frietag would have quite a row over the amount they wanted and what he offered. He always wanted to lend them less than he did the time before, because the things were getting 'vorn' or out of fashion. He'd say only fifteen shillings this week, and they'd say, 'Oh, please make it sixteen. I promise faithful to take them out next Friday.' Then after some more talk, 'Vell, I vill lend sixteen, but you will haf to take fifteen-and-six, and a quarter pound of tea.' (We kept a lot of packets of tea to sell in this way.) Then they would wail and say, 'Oh, no, Mr FriedEgg, please. I don't want tea. I want money for the rent and the grocer.' But they had to take it in the finish, so we got the interest on the sixteen shillings and the profit on the tea, as well as a penny for the pawn-ticket.

I didn't like to see little girls come in with things that their mothers had sent them to pledge. They looked so timid and ashamed, but Mr Frietag was more gentle with them, although he never lent them so much as they asked.

The pawnbroker's wife was a pretty lady with a lot of nice red hair. She used to talk to me when she was minding the shop while her husband had gone out to call on people who hadn't kept their promise to take things out on Friday. She wasn't a German Jewess, but came from Whitechapel in London, so Mr Frietag had to talk English to her. They had a dear little baby about eighteen months old who was called 'Izzy', which is a pet name for Israel. She let me nurse him on my lap sometimes when she was talking to customers. She could do business just as well as her husband, only she didn't make such a noise and wave her arms about like he did.

You can learn a lot of the value of things when you're in that trade, and what a difference there is between the price you bought them at and the money you get when you want to sell or pawn them. I remembered what 'Caveat Emptor' meant, and I think that's a jolly good motto to remember. Once when I had the chance, I looked at some invoices and saw what the pawn-tickets cost. It took me a long time to work it out, but I found that there was about eleven hundred per cent profit on them at a penny each. I also saw that they were printed at a place called 'The Land of Green Ginger, Hull'. I thought that was as funny as some of the Welsh place names.

Mr Frietag never gave me a direct order, but would only hint when he wanted something done. He'd say, 'Villiam used to do this', or 'Villiam did that.' Then he'd sigh and say, 'Ah, Villiam vos a goot boy — but he vos a tief.' I got a bit sick of hearing about William, so when I had nothing much to do I set about finding jobs. The shop front was like most of the shop fronts in Swansea, very dirty. So I washed that down and cleaned the shop floor. Then I made a lot of new tickets for the things in the window and that pleased him because he sold more goods.

It was fine to have Saturdays off and be able to go down to the docks and see the ships, but I liked best to go to the railway station and watch the mail train go off to London, always wishing I was on it and going back to Peckham. I often thought of my friends there.

We had a lot of wet days in Swansea, and when the weather was wet I found that I couldn't save the *Boys of England* for Sunday reading, but used it all up on Saturdays, so I took to going on Sunday evening to a large hall to hear the Christadelphians give addresses. It was awful to look at the big pictures they used to hang up and preach about. They had different ones every Sunday. One was of a giant with a head of gold, arms of silver, legs of iron and feet of clay and iron mixed. They said it was out of the Book of Daniel, and they felt sure that it was meant for Russia. England was having a quarrel with Russia just then and people used to go about singing a music-hall song:

We don't want to fight — but by jingo if we do,
We've got the ships, we've got the men,
And we've got the money too.
We've beat the bear before, and while our sons are true,
All the world shall never conquer little Britain.

47

We quite believed all that was true and felt very proud and puffed up about it, and that song gave the name of 'Jingoes' to people who want to go to war.

Some Sundays they showed pictures of horrible things out of Revelation. One was a great scarlet beast with seven heads and ten horns, enough to frighten anybody. I told our landlord, Mr Davies, about it, and he got interested and came with me every Sunday. They didn't have a collection at the Christadelphians, so that suited both of us. We used to talk about the things we had heard on our way home. I don't think he believed in it much more than I did, but we made out to each other that we did, and we wondered if Armageddon and the Millennium and the End of the World would happen in our time. The Christadelphians said it was coming soon. We thought it would be rather wonderful if we should see all those awful things, and if the world was going to bust-up it would be nice to be all together when it did and bust-up with it. Then we'd have a big laugh. At the same time I thought it might be safer to try to be a bit good and not tell many lies in case it came off.

Mr Davies was a fine big man with a fair curly beard like a Viking, and it was kind of him to be so friendly with me. He gave me good advice and had a lot of common sense although he had never been to school. He got his living by selling fish that he caught in his nets that were fixed in the sea a long way out, when the tide was at its lowest. Then the tide would come in and cover the nets ever so deep and when it went out again there would be a lot of different sorts of fish flopping about in the nets.

I got him to take me with him very early one morning before anyone was up, and as nobody would know I did it, I went barefooted. He wheeled his large barrow, and when we got right down to the nets we found lots of different sorts of fish left helpless on the sand, whiting, plaice, some conger eels and many smaller things that he threw over into the sea so that they would have another chance. He told me that when he was younger he used to go to sea for days together

48

in a fishing boat. He knew all about ships and showed me how to tell a schooner from a brig, and which was a barque and which was a full-rigged ship. Then he would ask me all sorts of questions about things he didn't know, and I believe I was able to teach him a little. He always wanted to learn more and was sorry that he couldn't read or write. Some nights I used to read the *Boys of England* to him and his wife. They liked that very much, so I used to show off and imitate the voices of the characters in the tales. Sometimes their little girl used to read to them out of her school books, but she couldn't do the long words. I liked sitting in their kitchen with them on Saturday and Sunday nights.

Then Monday morning would come again and people would roll in with things to pawn. Now and then a stranger would come in, and you could tell they weren't used to pawning. They'd always come to an empty compartment and speak in whispers. Sometimes you'd see a young man walking briskly by, and he would stop suddenly as if he was attracted by something in the window. He'd look closely at the watches and give a side glance up and down the street, and if the coast was clear he'd pop in and ask for ten shillings on a watch or ring.

Mr Frietag explained to me that it was always better to lend an odd amount because you got as much interest on nine shillings as you got on ten. So the young man had to be content with nine bob if the watch was worth thirty shillings. The interest was a ha'penny a month on every two shillings of the loan or less, so it worked out at 25 per cent a year. That's why he liked people to take the things out every week. He got a month's interest each time, which meant four times as much profit, besides the profit on four pawn-tickets instead of one. He said it 'vos goot business', and I thought so too and began to like him better. He was a very good husband too because after I had been there a few weeks he got me to do little things to help his wife. He said she wasn't very well, but she didn't look delicate to me, and I didn't know what was the matter with her until some time after. I had to go in the kitchen and lift the large kettle off the fire for her, and get things down from the top shelf of the dresser, and move many other heavy things that she asked me to, but all the time she was singing about the house and didn't seem ill at all. Soon after that he got a girl to come in and do those things and carry Izzy about, and I couldn't help noticing how kind Jews were to their wives because I'd never seen other husbands trouble much about what their wives had to do.

A few things happened soon after that made me alter my opinion of him. First of all he hinted that I should come in on Sunday mornings to help him because some people came then to take things out of pawn. He said that I had Saturdays off and I ought not to mind coming. 'Villiam vould haf come.' I told him that I didn't mind coming on Saturday but it would be wicked of me to work on Sunday, besides he didn't offer to pay me more for doing so. I didn't see why I shouldn't be as religious as he was, though he didn't use much religion on other days than his Sabbath, unless you counted his kindness to his wife, and even that broke down when money was concerned. I soon found that out.

One Friday evening he kept muttering to himself and looking at the clock, and at last he called his wife to mind the shop while he went to call on some woman who hadn't come to take things out like she'd promised. He hadn't been gone long before a gentleman came in and wanted to pawn a frock-coat. He asked twenty-five shillings for it and it was very good quality. After a lot of argument, Mrs Frietag lent him sixteen shillings on it. When Mr Frietag came back he looked very upset and angry and said that the woman had moved away and left no address. He said he had lent her more than he ought to have done on her faithful promise to redeem her things on Friday. He marched up and down behind the counter waving his arms and saying, 'It is ruin,' and that he would never get his money back, he would have to wait a year before he could sell them — if he ever did. He hollered at me for not picking up bits of string from the floor and tying them together. He raved so much that I thought he was going off his chump. Then he asked his wife if she'd done any business while he was away, and when he heard that she had lent sixteen shillings on a frock-coat he went properly mad. He shouted that frock-coats were quite unsaleable and 'You haf lent sixteen shillings — Mein Gott! He vill take it out neffer — nobody vill buy it, it is ruin.' He kept nagging at her like that for the rest of the evening, only leaving off when a customer came in. After they had gone he'd burst out again. I felt so cross that if I had been bigger I'd have landed him one for going on so at the poor woman. All the time he was nagging at her she never answered one word, but stood with her pretty head bent down like one of those slaves you read about in the *Arabian Nights*. If she had been a Welsh woman he'd have had a flat iron at his head! He was still at it when I left to go home. The last I saw of him he was leaning over the desk with his hands in his hair, muttering, 'Sixteen shillings for a frog-goat. Mein Gott.'

After that scene, I began to wonder whether the pawnbroking trade was a nice one to stop in. I didn't like the smell of that room where the pledges were kept, nor the long hours. I shouldn't like to have to be so hard to the poor people who wanted a little money so badly, or to the little children who came. I thought about those kids in the temperance procession and that made me see what a mistake I had made and what a fool I was. Of course, in a few years' time when those children grew up, nobody would drink beer and if people didn't spend money in public houses there wouldn't be so much need for pawnshops. That trade would be finished. What a chump! I told Mr Davies what I thought and he agreed with me, so then I looked out for something else, and this time I meant to find some trade that wasn't likely to go rocky. One large china and glass shop in Castle Street 'wanted a strong lad' and I thought that trade would be safe. When people gave up beer they'd want more cups and saucers. So I went in and saw Mr Primavesi. He was an Italian gentleman and very nice, and he spoke English quite well. He was doubtful about me because he thought I was rather small and not strong enough for the work. Heavy goods had to be taken out on a truck for delivery. I told him that I was much stronger than I looked, being short, and would he please take me for a week on trial. After thinking a bit he agreed to that and said I could start in a week's time and that he would pay me seven shillings a week if I suited.

Mr Frietag was rather cross when I gave notice, but he didn't offer me more money to stay on. I expect he thought he might get a new boy cheaper and save a bit that way. I wondered if he would tell the new boy 'vot a goot boy Tom vos', and he and Mrs Frietag were quite kind to me all that last week. One day she gave me a piece of fried fish — I had never tasted fish so nice before, and in a way I felt sorry to leave little Izzy and his mother. Some time after that I met her out, and she stopped and showed me a new little baby she had got.

When I found that Primavesi's closed at six and didn't open until nine, and also that they closed at one on Thursdays, I reckoned I was lucky to join that firm. Few of the other shops had such easy hours.

My first job every morning was to sweep out the shop and large show room and then dust the glass shades that covered beautiful ornaments and figures made in Dresden. They sold lots of things besides china and glass — guns, pistols, sword-sticks, instruments for seamanship, nasty-looking knives for sailors' use, and iron things that fitted over your fist, called knuckledusters. Some of the revolvers had handles made like a knuckleduster, so that if you missed shooting anyone you could bash him in the face with that. Sailors from foreign ships bought those things and the knives, and I thought things must be a bit lively in the countries they came from.

Captains from ships in the docks bought compasses, sextants and chronometers, but not very often. Some customers were gypsies and hawkers who bought cups and saucers and small plates at wholesale price to sell from house to house round the villages. We also packed many hampers of china things to go by railway to shops in all parts of Wales. Of course I didn't know all this the first week I came.

On the first day, after dusting, I had to go up to the warehouse at the top of the building and help a young man to get a large crate of china up from the railway van in the back lane. It came up by a crane and we had to turn a winch I don't know how many times before it came up high enough to be pulled through the warehouse doors. It was a slow job and very hard work. Now and then the young man put a brake thing on and stopped the winch so that we could have a rest. You had to be very careful in putting the brake on, because if you let go the handles of the winch when a load was on, they would fly back at a terrific speed and perhaps smash your face in.

Then we unpacked the crate and sorted out the plates and things in it and then stacked them on shelves. After that, orders came up and we picked out the different things on the lists and packed them in hampers with lots of straw. I was pretty tired and hungry when the one o'clock gun went off. This gun was near the docks and it was fired from Greenwich every day at one. You could hear it all over the town and everybody knew it was time to knock off for dinner. You would see people pulling out their watches and putting them right by the gun.

In the afternoon I had to get the truck out and take a load of plates up the hill to a large hall where they were to be left on hire for a large dinner-party. The plates were in four hampers and very heavy. I could only get along by pushing the truck about twenty yards and then taking a rest. It took a long time to get there like that, but it was downhill all the way back, so I ran with the empty truck. I was surprised that Mr Primavesi said I'd been quick. Next day I had to fetch them back and then it was the other way about. I had such a job to keep the truck from running away with me down hill, and I thought how awful it would be if it did and all those plates got smashed.

53

After the first time, I got to like going with loads of china to ships in the docks. Sailor men used to come and order dinner services with lots of extra plates, and large cups and saucers. I heard that crockery was very dear in the countries those sailors came from and when they were over in Wales they clubbed together and bought all they could. Then they smuggled it in to their own country and made a nice bit that way.

The first load I took was to a Greek ship in the South Dock. It was a barque and its name was *Michael Angelo*. Although the load was heavy it was easier work because it was downhill to the docks. When I got there I couldn't see any barque with that name, so I left the truck and walked up and down shouting '*Michael Angelo*, Ahoy' as I had been told to do, but no one answered. There were two ships in the middle of the dock, a barque and a brig, and I saw that the barque's name was printed in funny letters like zeds upside down and with ee's the wrong way about, so I thought that might be Greek. I shouted at the barque, 'Mike-Ell-An-Gel-O. A-hoy. A-hoy,' although it didn't sound much because my voice was a bit squeaky. Still nothing happened and I wished people would name ships with something simple and short, like they do dogs, not a crackpot mouthful like *Michael Angelo*. They might just as well call it *Christopher Columbus*, and how could anyone holler all that out? I did get wild. Then I thought that perhaps I should have to go back with the things and say I couldn't find the ship. What would Mr Primavesi say then? I was only on trial. Would I be kept on? I got so mad about it that I began to cry. Then I thought I would have another go, so I got a big dish out of the hamper and held it up in the air and danced about hollering. Some sailors from the ships there hung over the sides of ships and laughed, but two men from the ship with the funny letters got in a boat and rowed over to me.

The sailors took the hampers into the boat and got me to go with them to the ship. They were big thick men with brown faces, and one had little gold earrings. If they'd been dressed up for it they would have made good pirates, although they looked too friendly to be able to cut peoples' throats. When we got to the ship I had to go down with them to a smelly sort of place and unpack the things, while they counted them and saw that none were cracked.

There were six bunks down there and the place was very stuffy and dark. I wondered where they would find room to stow the china away and hide it. When everything was found correct they gave me two large ship biscuits, and one of them rowed me and the empty hamper back to the quay.

Two big boys were giving each other rides on my truck when I got on the quay, but they didn't start any rough game with me. They asked me if the sailors had given me any tobacco and said I ought to have asked for some. They told me always to ask for a lump of tobacco whenever I went to the ships and I'd be sure to get some. Then if I gave some to them they would push the truck for me; they knew where I came from and would watch out for me. That sounded pretty good, so I promised to do so but I didn't mean to give all of it away. I'd save some for Mr Davies. I told the young man in our warehouse about it and he said that all those sort of boys about the town chewed tobacco and would do anything to get a 'chaw'. I liked the biscuits, but they were very hard and I had to bash them against the wall before I could eat any. They wanted a lot of chewing but were good to stop you being hungry before dinner time.

Always after that I asked the sailors for tobacco, and they generally gave me quite a big flat lump of hard tobacco. Sometimes I got biscuits as well. When the ship was a French one, I said, 'Mercy,' to the sailors and 'Commong voo portay voo,' and that made them laugh. I'd cut the tobacco into smaller pieces and give one or two to any boy who would help me push the truck back. I generally saw one hanging about our yard. If I gave them an extra lump they gave me a ride all the way home on the empty truck.

On Thursday morning I had to go to the Weights and Measures Office and take a load of blue pint mugs to be tested and stamped. If they were correct they fixed a small band of lead round the handle and then the mugs were ready to be sold to country public houses. When I found that Primavesi's did a big trade with these and beer glasses I saw that I had been thinking all wrong again and perhaps had made another mistake, because when the temperance people shut up all the pubs, the mug and beer-glass trade would suffer. It seemed to me that it was no good thinking out things unless you'd got special good brains, and I thought perhaps it would be better to leave off thinking and leave things to chance or luck.

On Friday of the first week, I was given a job that I didn't like much. I didn't mind pulling truckloads of things about, but it was what I had to take that day that worried me. I had to deliver four hampers of chamber pots to a Girls' Home. They were made of white and yellow earthenware and I had nothing to cover them with. I had to wheel them as they were all naked-like through the streets. They had to go to a village outside Swansea and be delivered to a Girls' Home belonging to the Guardians where girls from the workhouse were trained to be servants.

Mr Primavesi gave me directions how to get there and said he'd been told it was three miles out. The things were not so heavy as a lot of plates so I could pull the truck easily, but people laughed at me, and boys who had nothing better to do walked along near me and made remarks. One boy asked me to lend him one for half a minute. They got tired of it after a time, and I got to the village all safe, but it seemed much farther than three miles. Then I found that the Home was a good way from the road up a long drive. As I went up I saw a sort of playground at the side where there were a lot of girls chasing each other about. One of them saw me coming and shouted out, 'Ooh, girls, here's a boy.' Then they all came running up like a lot of chickens at feeding time. I'd never seen such a mixed lot of girls, some dark and some fair, some half-and-half and gingery, and one with her hair quite red. They all looked happy and well-fed and some had rosy cheeks like apples.

But you wouldn't believe how those girls went on. They didn't seem to mind a bit about those things I had on the truck. They got round like flies and asked me if I made them and how much they were. They also asked how much they held and were really rude. One of them snatched my cap off and said, 'Who's your hatter?' and another wanted to know if my mother knew I was out. Then she ruffled my hair all up and said, 'Who curled your hair this morning, boy?' Then one said, 'Let's help him push the truck, girls,' and some of them got behind and pushed so that the truck moved very quickly, but after I'd gone a few yards they said, 'Whoa, Emma,' and pulled the truck back again. They did this twice till I got mad and hollered at them, but they only laughed and the red-haired one got behind me and pulled the back of my jacket up right over my head. I don't know what they'd have done to me if a tall woman hadn't come out and shouted, 'Now then, now then,' at them, and they scooted off like rabbits. I never did see such a cheeky lot of girls.

Thank goodness none of them was about when I came away, and as I went along I wondered whether girls always carried on like that when they were in a flock. I'd always thought that girls were shy and timid, easily frightened and ready to faint, like the young ladies in Mr Dickens's books, and I thought how awful it must have been for that Jewish king in the Bible who had a lot of wives all at once. I hoped they'd been better behaved than the girls in that Home. After I had gone a good way back, I saw a sign post that said it was four miles to Swansea, so Mr Primavesi must have been misled as he'd said the Home was three miles away. I knew that I had been a long time so I hurried as much as I could, running when I came to a down-hill bit.

It was past my dinner time but I had some ship biscuits in my pocket so that didn't matter, but I was tired when I got back. When I went in Mr Primavesi was very angry and spoke so crossly to me that it made me cry. I tried to tell him why I had been so long, but I couldn't. When he saw I was crying he turned kind at once, and said, 'That's all right. No, no. Don't cry. I didn't mean it. Yes, yes, forget about it.' I was so sniffy that I couldn't even thank him, and as I was too tired to go home to dinner, I went up to the warehouse and lay on the straw.

After that I thought Mr Primavesi was the kindest man I'd ever known and I was glad when he told me at the end of the week that I was properly engaged and could come regular. I was to bring a strong black apron to keep my trousers clean.

I was rather tired at the end of that first week and lay in bed late on Sunday and sat about reading until the evening. At this time some people named Dicks of Fleet Street, London, brought out all Sir Walter Scott's works complete at threepence each. They had yellow paper covers and small print. There was enough reading in one of those to last me a fortnight, so I gave up my twopenny papers and bought one of Scott's books every second week. That way I saved a penny — I know that sum is right, I worked it out on a piece of paper. I didn't like Scott's works as much as I did Stevenson's *Sea Cook*, but I learned a lot of history from them, and also got an idea of how ladies and gentlemen spoke to each other in olden days, and the right way to speak to a king if you met one. They were proper books for that sort of thing, and after I had read one all the way through I used to go through it again and read all the parts I had skipped the first time. You just couldn't help skipping parts when the tale got exciting. I liked the English stories best and thought *Kenilworth* and *Woodstock* were the best, but *Ivanhoe* was the most exciting. The barons used to carry on anyhow in those days. Fancy pulling out that old Jew's teeth to make him lend them money, and then never paying him back. I was glad I didn't know any barons if they acted that way. I liked to read about that young Jewess Rebecca, who nursed Ivanhoe when he'd got hurt fighting. She was so kind to him. If I'd a' been Ivanhoe, I wouldn't have married the fair Rowena. I'd rather have had a beautiful dark girl like

Rebecca, especially as she might have come into the old Jew's money later on, if the barons hadn't collared it all. You saw at the end of the book that although Ivanhoe was happy with Rowena, he couldn't help thinking of Rebecca now and then, as if he was sorry sometimes he hadn't had her instead. I expect it would have been just the same if he'd have married Rebecca — when he'd had a row with her he'd have got thinking of Rowena. Getting married is a bit of a toss-up when a man's got two nice girls like those hanging round.

People couldn't have been very busy in those days, or they wouldn't have had so much time for long conversations all full of long learned words, like they had in Scott's books, but perhaps Scott made it up, like when one gentleman meets a 'distinguished-looking stranger' on a heath or something, and gives him a 'courteous greeting' about it being a fine day and the stranger replies with a few 'well-chosen words' and finishes his remarks by quoting Latin. Then the first gentleman says, 'Sir, I perceive you are a scholar,' and he starts quoting Latin too. Then they both go on spouting Latin at each other. Perhaps it was the usual thing in those days, but I couldn't help thinking that Scott had put those bits in just to show off that he knew Latin, like I might do if I tried to write a book.

After I'd bought six of those books, I got the *Arabian Nights* for sixpence, and later on a complete Shakespeare for a shilling. Dicks of Fleet Street were jolly good people to print and sell books like those cheaply, so that poor people could get good things to read. I didn't need to buy any more, but read them over and over again.

Mr Primavesi spoke English and French quite well but he spoke his own language best and I liked to hear him and the Italian sailors bargaining for things. They talked so fast and loud that you'd think they were quarrelling, but they always finished up friendly. I learned a lot of Italian by listening when I was dusting. Primavesi was pronounced 'Prim-a-vasey' and if a thing was 'acquired direct from the producer' it was 'aquisitato directemente dal produttore'. If any article was 'genuine and superfine' it was 'genuino soprafino' in Italian. So it wasn't so very different from English and you could see that the words came from the same language, like Mr Bradley had told us they did.

When the summer was over, Mrs Primavesi and her little boy and girl came from their country house to live over the shop for the winter. Then I had to take the children to a convent school every morning at nine, and at mid-day take their lunch in a vegetable dish. It was always the same, just some macaroni with gravy on it — I could have eaten the lot in three mouthfuls. Then at four o'clock I fetched them home. They were nice children and very pretty, and we talked together as we went along. I told them bits out of the *Arabian Nights*, not the horrible parts to frighten them but tales like 'Aladdin and his Lamp'. So we got on well together and I made up my mind to learn all I could about the china and glass trade and stop there always. Pushing the truck got much easier and I didn't have any trouble to find the foreign ships. I discovered that hard work with your arms made you feel better than when you had to sit about writing envelopes and it made your arms and shoulders very strong. I found that out when I had to hit a boy once and he fell right over.

After I had been at Primavesi's for about three months, things at home got much better. Father got such a good name for selling things that many new firms in London sent goods to him for disposal to grocers and confectioners, so when I got home from work in the evenings I had to take parcels to shops that were not too far away. One thing that sold well was packet tea from the Bonus Tea Company in London. It was in quarter pound packets and labelled two shillings and sixpence a pound, and on the label it said that if any money was found in the packet it was a free present to the customer. It was a lottery really. The Tea Company knew that if a customer found a sixpence in her packet she would brag about it as if she had done something clever and tell all her friends and neighbours; then they would buy the tea, and it might have gone on and been a very big thing if the police in London hadn't stopped it. After that the firm must have gone broke because we never heard from them again. We had lots of the packets in stock that couldn't be sold because of the police, so as nobody asked for it back Father said it was 'fortune of war' and he needn't trouble about some commission they owed him.

I had to turn the tea out of the packets so that it could be sold loose to grocers, and it was quite true about money being in some of them. There was a brand new threepenny bit or perhaps a sixpence in one packet out of eight. I thought I might as well have a sixpence or so for myself, and I spent one of them to see the play *Othello* at the Theatre Royal, but I didn't tell anyone that I had been. I didn't like that play much, but I thought how well educated the people must have been in Venice all those years ago, to talk such beautiful language to each other. It seemed to me that Othello was a bit of a fool to believe all those things about his nice wife, and then go and kill her without giving her time to know what it was all about. I thought Iago was a nasty sort of chap, but he was good at thinking things out and everything seemed to come about just as he planned it — not like me when I think things. I liked what he said about 'putting money in your purse', though what that had to do with making Othello jealous I couldn't make out. I supposed that it was only a tale, and Shakespeare made it come about just as he wanted it to. Perhaps in real life Iago's schemes might have gone all wrong, like things do when I think them out.

I saved another of the sixpences until Christmas and went in the gallery of the Star Theatre to see a pantomime. I believe it was the first they ever had in Swansea, and Mr Melville's company that acted there all the year round took parts in it, and jolly good they were, too. Nellie Stanley acted as a boy; she sang fine songs and was very pretty with nice legs. Mr Emm was the comic man and he was very good at it and kept us laughing. About this time there was a great scare

61

in England about a beetle that had got over from America and might spoil all the potato crops. Everybody was talking about it. So in the Pantomime, the Demon King was dressed up to look like a beetle in yellow, with black stripes and spots. I can't remember all the words of his song, but I know the chorus because we all joined in!

> Take care of your little potatoes, boys,
>   And all your tiny spuds,
> Just watch your jolly cauliflowers,
>   And all your fuchsia buds.
> You'd better hide your bread and cheese,
>   And everything you've got —
> For the Colorado Beetle's come
>   To collar the jolly lot!

The fact that we were going to have pantomimes every year in Swansea did away with one of the reasons why I wanted to go back to London, but I still kept hoping. I wanted to see the old places in Peckham and the boys I used to play with. I didn't get on well with the Swansea boys. They were always fighting or playing rounders, but I couldn't talk to them for any time because they wouldn't believe anything I said. When I used to tell them about me going to college and having a shop in London with ponies and carts, they'd listen a bit and then say, 'There's a big liar you are.' When a Lord Mayor of London came down to open a new road, that made me think of Peckham again.

It was on early closing day, but the shopkeepers met and agreed not to open at all that day. The schools closed too, so it was a proper holiday. Even Mr Frietag shut up. Crowds came in from the villages around and we waited hours to see the Lord Mayor go by. I hollered and waved my cap as much as any of them because I looked on him as a neighbour of mine. He looked jolly fat and fine in his robes and cocked hat as he drove by in an open carriage, bowing and smiling as we cheered him. He was the same Lord Mayor that *Punch* made a joke about when he was elected. He was Alderman Stone before he was Lord Mayor, and *Punch* said, 'We hear that the new Lord Mayor has ordered that all the kitchen fat in the Mansion House be disposed of, because constant "dripping" wears away stone.'

7

Of course, just as I was settling down to learn the china trade, something had to happen. Trade was so good just then that Father's commission business got to be more than he could manage, so I was told to give Mr Primavesi notice to leave him and look after a lock-up shop that had been taken as a warehouse for the goods. It was to be called the Sale Room and money was going to be made 'hand over fist'. I had heard that said before, and didn't want to leave Primavesi's, but it was no use me objecting. When I told Mr Primavesi about it, he said he thought it was a pity because though I had to do menial work at present he had meant to put me in the show room later on to help sell things.

So I went to our Sale Room instead and had to wrap up parcels and deliver them to small shops. We had lots of different goods there. Boxes of confectionary, tobacco, nuts, sacks of oatmeal, packets of tea and lots of penny goods on cards, such as pills, bottles of castor oil, and worm tablets. I was pretty busy most mornings but some afternoons I had nothing to do, so I used to sprawl on the sacks of oatmeal and read Scott's books. One afternoon I drilled a hole in the side of a Spanish nut and then scraped the top off, breaking a lot before I succeeded. Then I fitted a clay pipe stem in the hole and made a tiny pipe, but it wasn't very satisfactory because the tobacco I smoked in it was Franklyn's Bristol Shag. I picked little bits of this out of the ends of the ounce packets . . . it couldn't have been the right sort to start smoking with, so I didn't do it again.

After a month or so trade got very bad owing to strikes and lock-outs at the works and mines. Shopkeepers couldn't pay their bills because their customers couldn't pay them, and many little grocers let the out-of-work customers have such a lot of credit that they were nearly ruined themselves. If we didn't get the money for the goods, there wasn't any commission or much work for me. I had to look out for another situation, but there didn't seem to be any boys wanted just then, only office boys 'quick at figures'. I got loafing about the town and docks again.

At home, I had to listen to a lot of talk about what I ought to do and didn't, and 'what I'd like to be when I was grown up', and 'what I'd be if I went on as I was doing'. I would have *liked* to be an artist and paint pictures, but there was a beautiful water colour painting of Oyster-mouth Castle in a shop window, better than anything I could hope to do. It was marked fifteen shillings and was there for a year without being sold. So an artist's trade wasn't much if you'd got your living to get. Other advice was to get a job in a shop where you lived in. 'Nothing like getting your legs under someone else's table. Then you can save best part of your wages and buy good clothes – If you've got a good appearance and plenty of cheek you can go anywhere – Put that book down and listen to me. Then if you're smart you can get better wages and if you save money you may have a shop of your own some day. But don't start in business without a good reserve of cash. That's where I made the mistake – I never had enough reserve. Always get your penn'orth out of everything and make up your mind to save money even if it's only threepence a week.' I never knew whether they meant it or not, especially about saving money, because they never did. I thought they might be 'getting at me' like they did when they told me about the parrots. I was rather dense and slow at grasping things because I remember them being surprised when I told them about what I had said to the people who bought those parrots. Then I thought things

65

would change.

An uncle of mine was manager of a colliery at Morriston where the men were satisfied and hadn't struck, and hearing that I was out of work he sent for me and said he had a job to suit me there. It was to sit in a small office that had a weighing machine connected with a weighbridge outside, and when trucks full of coal came on the weighbridge all I had to do was to look at the weighing machine and see what the weight was. Then take the weight of the truck when empty and so show what the weight of the coal was. It had to be entered in a book and chalked up on the truck. I was to have eighteen shillings a week and work from six in the morning until five at night, and half a day Saturday. It would have been an easy job for a boy quick at figures, but when they tested me it was hopeless. There were two of the bosses there as well as my uncle and I was so nervous with them looking on that I couldn't do anything with the figures. If I'd been alone I could have done it all right on a piece of paper, but it had to be done in the head and quickly. So I never went into the coal mining trade.

Every morning I made a round of the shops to see if boys were wanted and never missed looking in the window of Primavesi's. I would have asked to go back there if they had a vacancy, and I remembered how I enjoyed the work of dusting and cleaning up the china ornaments and beautiful cut-glass things. Best of all I liked the Dresden china shepherdesses with the pretty flowers painted on their dresses. I don't suppose shepherdesses ever did dress like that. If they did, looking after sheep must have been a cleaner job than attending to pigs. Then there were the little marble figures of white ladies, showing them as ladies are supposed to look when they've got nothing on. I didn't like them so well as the Dresden figures — they looked so cold — but they used to sell better than the others, and I expect I should have got to like them in time. Still, it was no use wishing. I couldn't expect him to sack his new boy to take me on again.

Then I saw an advertisement in the *Western Mail* for an

office boy in an accountants and debt-collectors' office. I applied for that by letter and got taken on straight away. But it was the shortest job I ever had, I got the sack after being there four weeks. Mr Fishwater paid me six shillings a week and the hours were nine till six. I had to address envelopes and fill in forms that threatened to do all sorts of nasty things to people if they did not forward something on account. But the debtors didn't seem to take any notice. The manager went out at eleven every morning to the saloon bar at the Castle Hotel and didn't get back until two o'clock, so I always went to dinner late. Some afternoons I had to take a list of addresses and go and call on people asking them to please pay something on account. But nobody did and some were quite rude to me and said what they'd do to me if I kept coming and knocking at their door just when they were having a nap, but they were ladies mostly. One man said, 'Give Mr Fishwater my respectful compliments and tell him to go to hell,' and another wished me to 'inform Mr Fishwater that he, the debtor, would be in Carey Street next Monday.' There wasn't a street of that name in Swansea, but Mr Fishwater seemed to understand.

After I had dusted and tidied up the office, I had nothing to do all the morning but wait for somebody to call and pay something on account. If other callers came, I was to say that he had gone to the County Court office, and if anyone paid any money, I was to give them a receipt out of a printed receipt book. But only one person ever did. One day after I had been there three weeks, an old man came and actually paid ten shillings off his bill. I was so excited at such an unusual thing that I wrote a receipt on the account he brought with him, and then just as he was going, I remembered the receipt book, so I gave him a receipt out of that too. He went off with two receipts for ten shillings, and when I told Mr Fishwater he gave me a week's notice.

That was the last job I had in Swansea, and leaving old Fishwater out of it, I'd had three situations in eighteen months. As there didn't seem to be any boys wanted anywhere except in offices, I got lazy and gave up looking. I spent my time down at the docks looking at the ships, listening to law cases at the Court in the Town Hall, and reading London newspapers at the Free Library. In the evenings, I played rounders and other games with boys in the field at the back of our house. Most of them were errand boys who came there after the shops were closed, but we generally had a row because they would not follow any proper rules in the games. I tried to get them to play the right way, but a big boy named Evans who was a good fighter used to call me a liar and always got his own way. He made up any rules that suited him and gave me a clump on the head. I think they only let me play with them because sometimes I put them up to some new mischief — we had many narrow escapes that way.

Except for the corner, there was no entrance to the field, as houses backed on to it all round. The field was only waste ground really and nobody seemed to use it but us. So it was a rotten thing of the owner to stack up a lot of railway sleepers across the place where the boys went in. He must have done it one morning, because when I went through the hole in our fence that evening, I was surprised to see no boys there. I went in again, and round to the road where the entrance used to be, and a lot of boys were there looking at the barrier and talking about it. The railway sleepers were about six foot high and fixed so close together that you couldn't squeeze through. Those boys were really wild and they even asked me what had better be done about it. Well, it seemed that that very night, when it was dark, all those sleepers were pulled up and carted away by somebody. Those who took them must have helped each other to lug them into each other's back yards and gardens. Those great lengths of tarred wood were very heavy. When they were chopped up into chunks, they burnt fiercely for a long time and saved a lot of coal. After that, the owner of the field didn't put up any more barriers, and we played every evening.

While reading the advertisements in the *Daily Telegraph*, I saw that there were so many Respectable Lads and Smart Youths wanted in different parts of London that I thought there couldn't be many boys out of work in London. I wondered whether I should stand a chance if I applied, so one day I wrote letters in reply and got one answer. It was from an oil and colour shop in north London, and they 'wanted a strong lad to do shop work and to be generally useful. One from the country preferred. Live In.' After one or two letters and references had been sent, they said I could come if I paid my own fare and I was to have five shillings a week and board and lodging.

I agreed to that and I was happy to know that I would be going back to London. I didn't have any trouble about it at home. 'The sooner the better.' Between us all, I managed to scrape up my railway fare. I had some sixpences and three-penny bits I'd saved up. Mr Davies made me have ten shillings and said I could pay him back when I'd made my fortune. He was very kind and I never forgot that I promised to write to him about how I got on. The night before I went, I packed up my best suit and other things and some of Scott's books in the carpet bag all ready, because the train started rather early next morning. Then I went into the field to have a last game with all the boys.

At first I thought I would tell them that I was going to London the next day, but changed my mind. They would only say I was a liar. After we had a few games and it began to get dark and time to go in, I got rather sad to think that I should never see those boys again. I wondered whether they would miss me and think of me sometimes and perhaps be sorry. Then I realized that I should never see Evans again and he could never clump me again, and that made me remember something my cousin Jack had tried to teach me. When Evans started being rough as usual, I sparred up to him. He was so astonished that he never guarded his face, so I punched him hard on the jaw and before he could get up I bunked indoors through the fence. He ran after me but didn't dare come in our garden because of Mr Davies, but he hollered a lot over the fence. Then he went round to the front door and shouted things through the letter-box. 'All right, Tom Lloyd, I'll get yer. You wait. I'll knock yer stuffing out tomorrow.' Swear words as well, and awful things that he'd do to my liver. Mr Davies had to go out and chase him away.

They asked me what I'd done to the boy and I said 'nothing' but they wouldn't believe me, and said, 'Why do you associate with such boys? Such language!'

The train started at eight but I got to the station long before
that and I met a man there who lived next door to us. He
used to go up to London every day sorting letters in the mail
train. He spoke to the Guard about me and the Guard said he
would put me on the right road when we got to Paddington.

It was a slow train and stopped at every station, and
although I got hungry I didn't like to get out my sandwiches
before the other people in the carriage. They sat there silent
and looked at each other now and then as if they were
enemies. I had a seat in the middle so I couldn't see much of
the scenery except watching the telegraph poles flash by.
Every now and then I thought of Evans waiting and looking
out for me that evening and night after night after that, and
it made me laugh right out. The people in the carriage must
have thought I was going off my chump.

Then I'd think that perhaps it was not a nice thing for me
to have done. We ought to forgive our enemies and turn the
other cheek. But Evans never cared whether you forgave him
or not, it made no difference. If you had turned the other
cheek to him he'd have socked that too. So perhaps it was as
well that I had got level with him like I did. I wished I'd
been able to think out artful things to do to him like Iago
did in *Othello* — I might have got square with him some other
way and hurt him more. Of course, Ivanhoe wouldn't have
done like I did. He'd have fought it out no matter how big his
enemy was — but Ivanhoe was all dressed up in ironmongery

and rode on a horse. He also had a long pole to keep the other chap off. It wasn't like that in my case. So perhaps it was all for the good, and I was more glad than sorry. What with thinking things like that, and going to sleep for a bit, and laughing now and then, the time passed pleasantly enough, and we got to Paddington about four in the afternoon.

The Guard showed me where to wait for a bus to Hornsey, but before I left the station I sat down and had something to eat and some water from a drinking fountain. I had a long walk up a hill from the place where the bus put me down and had to sit on my bag and rest once or twice. Then the road went downhill and I soon found Mr Frogmarch's shop. It was the end one of a row of shops, a grocer next door, then a porkbutcher and farther on a baker.

When I told the young man in the shop who I was, he took me into a parlour behind the shop and showed me to a very old gentleman who had a long white beard. There were three rather oldish ladies there sitting down, and it looked as if they had just finished tea. The old gentleman asked me about the shops I had worked at and one of the ladies asked if I had done any housework. I told her that I didn't mind what I did and they said, 'That's the way to get on.' One of them put some water in the teapot and gave me a cup of tea and some bread and butter and took me out into a kitchen where I had it. After that I had to go outside the shop and keep an eye on the things that were laid out on the pavement. There were dozens of pails, zinc baths, brooms and brushes, kettles and heaps of other iron and tin things. A boy was standing outside the grocer's shop next door looking after and selling eggs which were in long boxes laid out on the pavement. He came near and asked me where I had come from, and when I told him I came from Peckham where my father had a grocer's shop he said I was a liar, that nobody talked like I did in London. Then I knew that after living four years in Wales I had got to talk with a brogue like the Welsh boys did when they spoke in English. I didn't like that too much.

72

The shop closed at nine and I had to start carrying all the things in at half past eight, and then put up the shutters. They gave me some bread and cheese in the kitchen and later on one of the ladies showed me where I was to sleep. It was a small bed in the corner of a front room where the young man slept. She said I could go to bed as soon as I liked and she would wake me at a quarter to seven and show me what I had to do before the shop opened at eight. I was very tired and soon went to sleep, but there weren't enough clothes on the bed. In the morning I had to clear out the ashes in the fireplace, blacklead the stoves and light the fires. Then the lady said, 'Clean yer master's boots,' and after that I had to scrub the kitchen table. Then I had a wash and carried the things out on the pavement again, after taking down the shutters.

By this time it was nine o'clock and they called me into the kitchen to have breakfast. I had a cup of coffee and three lumps of bread and butter. It was rather stale and leathery but I enjoyed it. After breakfast, I had to take a basket and deliver soap and things to customers, and call on a list of places for orders. I had a job finding the houses but a boy who worked at the baker's was delivering bread, and he kindly told me how to find them.

Some of the customers asked me what part of the country I came from, and one said, 'How many more boys is Frogmarch's going to have?' When I said why did she ask, she told me that they had had six boys in the last three months and that local boys wouldn't work for them. I said, 'Perhaps the boys are no good and afraid of work.' I thought the Frogmarch's were very nice people and I'd stop with them all right. She said, 'Ah! We shall see.' Then at another house two young ladies came to the door and after they'd taken in the oil and soap one of them said, 'How's your manager this morning?' And the other one said, 'When you get back, ask him if he's ready.' I expect they must have wanted someone to talk to; some of the ladies were like that. They'd keep you jawing and then not give you an order. When I got back, I

73

had to mind the shop while the manager went in to dinner, and call him out if anyone came in. Afterwards I went in for mine, and a very good dinner it was. In the afternoon, there were more goods to take out and then I had a lesson in mixing paint. When anyone wanted paint it had to be made up for them while they waited, so much white lead and so much linseed oil, turpentine and dryers. If they wanted it coloured, I had to add dry powders or oily colour in paste form. I tried to learn all I could because I found out that the profits in the oil and colour trade were very good. When travellers called, I listened to the prices they asked and then compared them with what we charged. We made three ha'pence profit on a pound of yellow soap and many other things paid better than that.

My work went on like that from day to day, and I was always busy except in the evening when I had to stand outside and watch the goods. I asked the manager if he'd let me paint the prices on the pails and things with whitening or blue, and when I did it, it brightened the things up no end. After that, I often sold a kettle or a frying pan from outside the shop.

The first Saturday, they asked me if I would rather stay there on Sunday or have a shilling and go away all day and keep out until nine o'clock. Of course, I said, 'Yes, please,' and on Sunday I cleared off early. I found that I could get all I wanted to eat and yet save something out of that shilling.

Some Sundays I went to Regents Park, near the zoo. I heard the animals howling and once I went close to the gates of the zoo and saw a notice there asking Fellows of the Zoological Society not to take in any person who might accost them. That gave me an idea, and when I saw a gentleman coming along to go in, I asked if I might go in with him. He said, 'No, boy, certainly not,' so I was sorry I had taken my cap off to him. I felt afraid to ask any more men, but after I had hung about a bit, a pleasant-looking short fat man came along, so I thought I'd have another try. He looked at me rather funny and said, 'What part of Wales do you come from?' I was astonished, but he said he knew directly I'd opened my mouth. He was a doctor from Cardiff, up for a short holiday, and he said I could come in with him and everything would be all right.

I did have a fine time that Sunday. The gentleman took me all round and showed me the animals and birds, talking and explaining things all the time. He asked me questions about who I was and what I did for a living, and things like that. I told him about Swansea and what had happened there and about the pigs, and when we went in the parrot-house I told him about those parrots we sold, and he did laugh! At one o'clock he said, 'What about lunch?' and took me to the dining place and gave me a nice dinner. Then we saw the lions fed, and the sealions having fish, and later on we had tea with cakes. After tea he said he had to be off, so he shook hands with me and in his hand was half-a-crown which he put into mine. I'd never met such a kind man, and I was glad I'd seen that notice on the gate. I thanked him a lot and said I wished I could do something for him in return for all that money. He laughed and said, 'When you come to Cardiff you can clean my brass plates.' I promised him I would and asked for his address. He laughed again and said his name was Galen and he lived at Mount Olympus.

I expect there are many kind people about like him if you know where to look for them, but I never found one again near the gates. I tried several times after that but I never got anyone to take me in again, and at last the man in the ticket office came out and chased me away. After that, I left off going.

About this time, a new Sunday paper called the *Referee* came out. It had lots of good reading about theatres and parliament, but best of all was a page of funny writing called 'Mustard and Cress' by George R. Sims. I bought this every Sunday and it lasted me all the morning in the park or wherever I could find a place to sit down, but I always threw it away before I got home because Frogmarch's were so religious. When the weather was wet I went in any church that was handy and after the services went on to the nearest coffee shop. I stayed there as long as I decently could and read the *Referee* there. When the coffee shop people began to look rather funny at me, I went off to another place and had a small cup of tea or coffee and looked at *Punch* and other papers they had there for customers' use. I never once met anyone to talk to; the girls in the coffee shop were always too busy. If I started talking to one of them about the weather or something, she'd say, 'Yes. Anything else? That'll be fourpence.' That was how I spent Sundays until it was time for the long walk home so as to be back by nine o'clock for prayers.

On my way back, I used to think how horrible it was that Monday morning was coming again, with another long week of work without a break until Sunday came again. The only time I went back happy was the day I met that kind fat doctor.

Soon after I got in, I had to go in the back parlour where all the others were, except the manager, and sit down while old Mr Frogmarch read some scripture. After that we turned round and knelt down on the floor with our heads down and our elbows on the seat of the chair. That old gentleman could pray well. There seemed no end to the things he wanted. Then he'd pause and I thought he'd finished, but he hadn't. He'd think of other things he wanted and go on and on until I felt I was getting the cramp. Then at last he said, 'Amen.' None of us got up at once but seemed to be waiting for the others to make a move. It was awkward having our backs to him. You couldn't open one eye a bit and see if the others were getting up, like you can in church. The manager, who was a nephew of Mr Frogmarch, never came in to prayers. I never knew what time he came to bed, except once when he tumbled against the washstand and I woke up and heard the clock downstairs strike two.

The boy at the grocer's shop told me that our manager went off every night to the Angel at Islington. I don't know how he knew, but perhaps he'd heard the grocer talking. He told me too that our manager had been locked up a little time ago and had been taken to the police court next day. He said some girl had been locked up at the same time and the things the policeman said about them made everybody laugh, and when it was in the paper next day all Hornsey was laughing about it. Then that boy said if I wanted to get on the right side of the manager and make him kind to me, I was to ask him if he was ready. 'Just say, are you ready, that's all. You'll see.' I couldn't understand what it all meant and I didn't think I wanted to do what that boy said. It seemed so mysterious and maybe he was up to some Iago sort of game.

Something strange happened in the middle of one night after I had been there two months. I woke up hearing an awful row in the room. He had got the window open and was leaning out and shouting, 'Police! Murder! Thieves!' over and over again. I was very frightened and covered my head with the clothes. Then the three old ladies came running in one after the other, so I felt safer and peeped. They were in long nightdresses and two of them had black shawls over their heads and the other had a patchwork quilt over her. They looked to me like the witches in *Macbeth*.

Then there was a knocking at the door just like there was in that play. One of the witches went down and brought up a policeman. He looked all over the room and under my bed but he didn't find any murderers. He asked me if I'd seen anything, and all the time the manager sat on his bed with his hands over his eyes, crying out, 'Keep them off. Take them away,' whenever the policeman spoke to him. When he'd calmed down a bit they got him to go to bed and the ladies tucked him up. One of them said, 'Would you take a glass of sherry, officer?' and took the policeman downstairs. So everything was quiet again, and I went off to sleep, but I felt jolly glad we had separate beds in case he often had dreams like that.

They never mentioned anything about it next morning,

and I said nothing either, but they gave me a whole egg for breakfast and as I'd never had anything but bread and butter before, I wondered if they had done it to keep in with me like, so that I shouldn't talk about it to people outside.

I wouldn't have done in any case. I might tell lies now and again, but it's rotten to be disloyal to the people you work for and who pay you well. You ought to stick up for your firm and not let people run them down, and another thing, I might have got the sack if I went about talking.

When they sent me next door for tea and sugar the grocer wanted to know all about the row last night, but I didn't answer him. I kept staring at him vacantly as if I didn't understand. He soon gave it up, but he did look cross and as I went out he said I was a brainless pup. In the evening, when we were both minding goods outside the shops, the grocer's boy wanted to know all about it, but I told him to mind his own business, and that made him wild. He called me frogface and said for two pins he'd swipe me on the jaw. After that, I began to think I should have trouble with that boy.

Before I went to bed that night, I wrote a letter to Mr Davies in Swansea and told him how I'd got on, and about the doctor at the zoo. I knew he'd be interested because he used to get his little girl to read to him things that I had written in exercise books — I used to jot down things I had seen or done — and he'd asked me to write bits like that to him. Next day I got a post office order for ten shillings and put that in the letter too. I had saved quite a lot of money, over a pound. My washing cost eightpence and paper collars threepence a week, and the only other money I spent was for a penn'orth of broken biscuits now and then. I kept a bit in hand for boot mending and things like that, but I put away half a crown every week and wouldn't touch that for anything. I kept my best suit clean for Sundays; it didn't matter much about the other things in the week because a big apron covered those and kept off the splashes of paint and oil. We sold a lot of paint at spring cleaning time, but Good Friday was the time. We kept open until eleven in the morning and men came for more and more paint and I had to go on mixing it until I got sick of the job. The fat-headed lot seemed to have nothing better to do on Good Friday than painting up the dog kennel or the summer house or something. We lent them pots and brushes free. The paint pots were made of red earthenware; they were round with a little handle at the side, like those things I took to the Girls' Home, only smaller.

When we shut at eleven, I went and put my best clothes on so as to go out for the day, but before I got away, more painters came knocking at the door and I had to go down in the cellar all dressed up and mix more paint for them. I felt so cross about it that I would have liked to empty a pot of paint over their blooming heads, so that when I did get away I was disagreeable. They didn't give me an extra shilling for going out all day like they did for Sundays, and there wasn't any *Referee* either, so I didn't enjoy myself much that day, but at least I didn't have to work.

By this time, I had learned a lot about the trade and made up my mind to always be an oil and colour man. The only thing I didn't like was that they didn't keep biscuits and other eatable things like grocers did. I liked standing outside and selling things, but best of all I liked the job of painting the prices on them. I admired the figures I drew, but I never heard anyone else do so.

Many times when I was busy, the grocer's boy annoyed me a good deal, saying rude things and calling me frogface and 'country Joskin'. He was a tough-looking boy so I ignored him, and that made him worse. As I liked someone to talk to, I made friends with the baker's boy when I met him on our rounds. One evening when I was stooping down and writing '9d.' on a kettle, someone threw an onion that hit me on the neck. I knew it must have been that grocer's boy because there wasn't anyone else about, but when I looked at him he was eating peas-pudding out of a paper and looking straight across the road at a dog. So I couldn't prove anything.

A little later I went inside to get some more water to mix

with the colour I was using, and when I came out I saw that peas-pudding had been thrown on the kettles that I had just been doing. So that settled it. I didn't want any more proof and I lost all my temper and went round and punched at that boy. I couldn't hit him under the jaw like I wanted to; he kept putting his hand up and hitting out at me. I hit him back but we didn't hurt each other much, but somehow when we were struggling, he fell backwards into a box of eggs, so I went back to our shop.

The grocer came out and went in to our shop and carried on about it to my manager. The manager had an awful headache that day and he said, 'Oh, damn the boys, don't come bothering me.' The grocer said, 'Your boy deliberately committed an unprovoked assault on my boy, and what about my eggs?' I said, 'What about peas-pudding?' and he said, 'You shut up,' and went on again at the manager. It was a pity about his headache; I expect that's why he swore at the grocer. Then the grocer started swearing and I hoped they were going to have a scrap too. Old Mr Frogmarch came out from the back parlour and kept saying, 'Sssh, sssh,' because of the language, but the finish of it was that they agreed that it was my fault and I would have to pay for the broken eggs or else get the sack. The grocer went and counted them and then came back and said two shillings. So I had to pay that out of my saved money, and that made me more mad than ever. I couldn't go to sleep for a long time that night thinking of it and what I'd do to that boy when I caught him somewhere away from his shop. And I did reckon that the manager was a measly cad to roach on me and not stick up for one in his own firm.

When I went outside next evening, that boy didn't say anything to me. The back of his trousers were stained and shiny through sitting on the eggs, and I kept looking at that part of him as if I was examining a strange animal at the zoo or a Colorado beetle. Then I stepped back a bit to get a better view of his trousers and kept staring intently at them. I could see that he was getting more and more wild and I hoped that he would come over to my ground and assault me. Then if he fell over, he'd know all about it because of the iron things there. But he didn't do any more than look wild, so I had to think of some other way.

Other shop boys heard about it and got interested. I told the baker's boy about what I'd do to the grocer's boy when I caught him away from the shop, and he told the others and some of them told the grocer's boy. After that, I never seemed to meet him like I used to do, and if it hadn't been for that two shillings I might have forgotten about it. Then I heard that he had told other boys that he was going to half murder me — the baker's boy told me that — but still we never came across each other when we were out. Some of those boys went out of their way to make themselves busy. One day two of them told me that he had just gone up Pinecliff Road with goods and if I waited a bit I could get him. But as I told them, I was in a hurry to get back as I had been told to be quick.

Then one morning when I was going up Hearburn Avenue with the baker's boy, we saw that grocer's boy coming in the distance. I had to keep going because that other boy was there; he got quite excited and said, 'I'll hold your jacket.' I thought I'd have to go through with it, like you do at the dentist's, so I threw down my basket and tore off my coat, and started tucking up my sleeves and waiting for him to come near. When he saw what I was doing, he stopped and turned back as if he had forgotten something. We both ran after him and when I got near he said, 'Don't hit me. I'll give you best.' I couldn't do anything after that, so I never really got level with him after all, but I did kick his basket into the road. The baker's boy was rather disappointed, but he told the other boys what had happened and I never had any trouble with boys after that. Anyway, it shows what bluff can do. If he'd have stood up to me and I hadn't had the luck to get him under the jaw quickly, he could have whacked me easy, because no matter how mad I was I always soon had enough.

After I had been with Mr Frogmarch about nine months, things began to happen that made me start thinking again. The old gentleman got a man in to take stock and I don't think it could have come out very well. They went about looking worried and I heard Mr Frogmarch talking quite angry to the manager. The thin old lady who ordered me about got more and more irritable and found more housework for me to do. I didn't have so many goods to take out as I did when I came first and the orders I got were hardly worth collecting. I don't think customers liked that manager much. I always had to wash the towels I used and I did my handkerchief at the same time, and I must have done them rather well because she brought me dusters to do and things that they used to send to the laundry. I had to soap and boil them, and sometimes I had quite a pailful. I didn't mind because it was a nice warm job, and while I was doing that I wasn't doing anything else.

The only thing was that she would keep poking about and watching me, and every time I splashed soap-suds about or dropped water on the floor, she nagged. She never lost a chance to nag at me, especially when someone had upset her. She had never been married, and not having any husband to jaw at when she felt like it, she let it off on me. Sometimes when she was in a tantrum, I tried smiling kindly at her, but that made her worse.

The food wasn't so good as it had been at first, either, and not half as much as I wanted, but it got worse than ever when old Mr Frogmarch was taken ill and stayed in bed. The doctor came every day and ordered him beef-tea, so there was always a saucepan of that stewing on the fire. Then they had the cheek to give me the bits of stewed beef for my dinner. They were like pieces of rag with no goodness left in, and no more flavour than blotting paper. I didn't mind the first time, but they kept on giving me the same thing every day, so I began to wonder whether the old gentleman would die soon or keep on being ill.

One day I left my dinner untouched and went next door.

I bought some broken biscuits and ate them instead. When she asked me what I meant by leaving my dinner and how dare I go out without permission, I told her that I didn't want that sort of dinner; I'd rather eat coke. She went off and told the manager what I had said, and he swore at me and said that I deserved to be discharged at a minute's notice for impertinence. Then I got cross too, and said I would give them a week's notice and leave.

When I went in to tea, she said that they had been thinking of giving me notice for a long time, but I went on chewing and said nothing. So when my time was up, I packed my things in the old carpet bag and went off to Peckham.

I'd always wished to go back to Peckham to see the old places and my friends, so when I knew I was leaving Hornsey, my first thought was to go there. I'd got a bit of money saved to carry me on until I got work in some shop, and if I did I wouldn't go away from Peckham any more. I walked a good bit of the way and then got on a tramcar; it didn't go very fast but you went an awfully long way for tuppence. Two poor mules pulled it along and people kept getting off or on, so those poor animals had to strain hard to start it going again. When I got to Peckham, I went to the part where working people lived and left my bag at a sweet shop where I bought twopenn'orth of 'cokernut' candy. You could get a quarter of a pound for tuppence; and there's a lot of chewing in it when you're hungry.

After that, I went and looked about for lodgings, and after a bit I found a place that looked clean, a small cottage in Sumner Road, double-fronted with a long garden in front and none behind. There was a tiny furnished bedroom over the wash-house to let at three shillings a week, so I paid the first week's rent at once and went to fetch my bag.

The lady at the cottage said that her husband worked at the goods office at Bricklayer's Arms station on night work, and he could always wake me up early in the morning when he came home, if I wanted him to. When I unpacked my bag I found that my best suit had got creased, so I hung it up, and then I put my boots on the mantelpiece. I thought that the little room did look nice and cozy. When I went out again, I found a nice coffee shop in the High Street where I had a good cup of coffee and two slices of bread and butter, all for fourpence ha'penny. Then I went off to look at our old shop, but it looked much smaller than it used to be, and wasn't a grocer's any more, but a tinsmith's. The greengrocer had gone and so had the chemist where Harold Warren used to live. It seemed that I wouldn't see any of the boys or people that I used to know anywhere about there, so I walked about for a long time, and went under the railway arches where we used to play, but there was nobody there. The whole place looked dismal and mouldy to me, and I got dismal too. I thought that perhaps all my friends were dead and gone, and I thought of coffins and measles and things that bring you out in spots, and of Nunhead Cemetery. So I almost wished I had not come back to Peckham, but it was more cheerful up Rye Lane. There were many more shops than there used to be, and very few private houses left, and what there were had doctor's brass plates on the gates. As I went along, I looked to see if any Respectable Lads were wanted. I called at two pawnbrokers and told them that I knew all about the trade, but they had no vacancy for a job. It was the same at an oil shop and a large china and glass store. There wasn't any brewery up Rye Lane. By then I was so tired, I went back to Sumner Road and went to bed.

After having breakfast at that coffee shop, I went up Rye Lane and bought a strong box to keep my clothes and things locked up. It cost four shillings and sixpence and was grained and varnished outside, and the inside was lined with pretty wallpaper. After I'd carried it to my lodging, I went out and tried to sell my carpet bag, but the man at the second-hand shop said it wasn't fashionable and I'd better take it away and burn it. I took it home again and wondered what I'd better do with it; I never thought to ask the landlady if I could put it in her dust-hole, so I took it out late that night, but couldn't drop it anywhere. Someone always came along just as I was going to shy it over into a garden of an empty house, or on to a bit of waste ground. No matter how deserted a road was, directly I tried to plant that bag the place became alive with people. It was like those dragon's teeth I'd read about — whenever you sowed one, an armed man sprang up. I stood on the canal bridge looking over, but then a policeman came along. Next day, I took it up Rye Lane to the Rye, and sat with it on a seat there. A good many people were about on the Rye, but nobody called after me when I got up and walked away without that bag! I wondered whether some honest person would find it and take it to the police station.

Each day I went through all the streets where the shops were, and looked to see if boys were wanted. Then I got up very early and read the wanted advertisements in the paper at the coffee shop, and some days I walked miles after one of those jobs, but there were many other boys waiting outside the shops and by the time I got in the job was gone. I had enough money to last me eight weeks if I was careful, but as week after week went by I got anxious. I wouldn't write to Wales and tell them, in case I'd have to go back there, and I didn't want to go there any more than they wanted me. I'd rather take any sort of job I could get, or else starve, or go in the workhouse. I thought of the jolly girls at the Swansea Girls' Home, how well fed and happy they looked and I wished I were a girl. Poor boys had a rougher time than girls and didn't get as much pity.

I always went home rather early every night, and read my books in bed. Once I burnt the landlady's candle all away. She didn't say anything about it, but she put smaller bits after that. I got to like that lady; she was quite a young woman, like a big girl really, and she had a baby girl about a year old. After a time she let me go in the kitchen in the evening and sit by her fire while she talked about Laleham, the village where she came from. She would talk right on for ever so long while I sat quiet and listened. I kept looking at her while she talked, and noticed how pretty she was, with such nice rosy cheeks, quite unlike most of the Peckham people. I only saw her husband on Sundays. He was a nice man and not old at all. He was fond of reading but hadn't many books, so I lent him some of my Scotts — by then they were very greasy and dirty, but he didn't mind. In return he lent me a book by Darwin about earth worms. It was rather dry at first, but not having anything fresh to read I stuck to it and got to like it. I learned a lot about those worms and the good they did to the ground by bringing up the soil from underneath and making the surface fertile. I thought that everyone with a garden ought to read it, and then they'd think twice if they chopped a worm in half when they were digging. Perhaps it's a good thing not to be able to buy many books, so that if you can afford only one good book you have to make that last a long time and read it over again. That way you remember all you have read in it. I thought that it was something like a lump of bread and cheese to a hungry man. That would do him more good than a big dinner of lots of different stuff would do to a man who was rich and fat.

While I'm telling you about Mrs Pagles, my landlady, I may as well put down other things that happened while I lodged with her, even after I got work at a boot shop, and I'll tell you about the boot shop later on.

Some nights the landlady would go up and fetch her baby down if she heard it crying, and let me nurse it on my lap for a bit. She said she was glad to have me in the kitchen of an evening as she didn't know anyone in Peckham, not to talk to. Her husband being away all night and going to bed in the day when everything had to be kept quiet didn't give her much chance to talk as much as she would have liked to do. I thought it was a funny way to go on, and I shouldn't have liked it if I was married, but she seemed very happy and made an awful fuss of that baby.

She told me that it was hard to get nice lodgers because her cottage didn't look up to much outside, but it was nice and clean inside and I told her that it was her clean windows and nice white curtains that attracted me when I was looking for a room, and that directly I saw her when she opened the door I knew I should be happy in her house. Then she seemed ever so pleased. She had another room to let, a much larger one than mine; the rent was three and six a week and she said that if she was lucky enough to get another lodger she would let me have the bigger room at the same rent as I was paying. I thought about that for a bit and then said that if I went about and got her another lodger would she let me stop where I was for sixpence a week less, and that perhaps I might get her one who would pay four shillings. So she agreed to that and made me a cup of cocoa.

I was glad I had found such nice people to live with, and perhaps it was a good thing for them too that I was lodging there, because once she came into my room in the middle of the night not dressed up or anything. I was frightened when she woke me up and I saw her standing there in her white night-dress like a ghost. Then I saw that she was in great trouble and crying. She was sobbing so that she could hardly speak properly, but kept bringing it out in bits. 'Oh, my babby — what shall I do? It's going to die — oh, my dear babby!' So I put my trousers on and went with her to her room. That little child was in a fit or something, and it looked blue. Its little hands were clenched and there was froth on its mouth and it kept sputtering instead of breathing properly. I looked at it but didn't know what to do about it, and all the time that girl cried and said, 'What shall I do?' and wiped the tears away on her nightdress. Then I remembered something I had read somewhere about kids in convulsions. I didn't know what convulsions were to look at, but that book said that a warm bath was good for them. So I said, 'There, there — don't cry. Everything will be all right,' because I thought that it wouldn't do the baby any harm to have a warm bath even if it didn't cure it. I ran down to the kitchen and made a big fire with newspapers and bits of wood, and soon had a kettle of warm water. Then I took it up and got her to take the baby's things off. It was a job to get her to do it properly, she kept fumbling about and crying, but she managed it at last and we put the warm water in a tin bath from under the bed and laid the baby in it. She held its head and shoulders while I poured warm water on the little thing's chest. Well, you wouldn't believe, but in quite a short time it stopped making funny noises and began to breathe properly. It stretched out its little legs and opened its eyes and then began to yell out like babies do and seemed all right again.

But that girl wouldn't leave off, she kept crying all the time she was drying it, but perhaps she was crying for joy then. After a while the baby went to sleep and I said I would go to bed again, but she kept on thanking me so that I thought I should never get away. She wanted to make me a cup of cocoa, but I wouldn't let her. When the husband came home next morning, she told him about it and he came and shook hands with me and looked as if he was going to start crying too. All that fuss because I'd remembered something I'd once read! They both said that they would never forget it, and I didn't forget it either, because I'd never seen a baby girl with nothing on before.

I'll leave off now about Mrs Pagles, and tell you how I got the job at a boot shop. My money was nearly all gone and I got so anxious that I gave up looking for notices in shop windows but went in shops up and down Rye Lane and asked if they wanted a boy. Some did but they wouldn't pay more than five shillings a week. 'We can get plenty of boys for that.' But I kept on calling and at last I had the luck to get engaged as a shop boy at a shop in Rye Lane kept by a Mr Kenelly. He was more of a gentleman than any of the other shopkeepers and spoke kindly. He asked me about what shops I had worked at and I told him about them all, and also that once we had a grocer's shop in Peckham and I knew a good deal about that trade. He seemed very interested and said that he had been a grocer too but had given it up and gone in for boots because there was more profit in the boot and shoe trade. He joked about it and said, 'What's the price of Common Congon now?' meaning cheap China tea. Perhaps if I hadn't been a grocer I wouldn't have got that job. He told me to start on Monday, and he would pay me eight shillings a week. He never troubled about references.

So then I had to think out how to live on eight shillings a week, and I worked it out as best I could. My breakfasts at Colepeter's coffee shop came to two shillings and eightpence a week, rent and washing cost three and eightpence, and that left only a shilling and some pennies for dinners and tea. So the first thing to do was to make breakfast cheaper. I bought a little spirit stove and a tiny kettle for ninepence the lot, some methylated spirit in a medicine bottle for threepence, a loaf of bread for tuppence three farthings, and some beef dripping which I kept in an old jam jar, for fourpence. A tuppenny packet of cocoa lasted me a week and as it was a thick sweety kind I didn't have to buy any milk or sugar. There was plenty of room in my clothes box for them, so I kept the lot there so that Mrs Pagles shouldn't see them. Every morning after that I'd light the stove first thing and by the time I'd finished washing, the water was boiling ready for making a cup of cocoa. Then after breakfast I packed the things away in the box and locked it up. I reckoned that I saved one and six in a week by doing things that way. Later on I saved another ha'penny on two loaves of bread a week by going up to the Old Kent Road where a new German baker was selling bread at tuppence ha'penny the loaf. This way I had three shillings and tuppence for the rest of the week and I had to make it do till things got better. If I had a good dinner on Monday such as a beefsteak pudding, fourpence, potatoes, a penny, and a pennor'th of rice pudding after, a penny cup of coffee and a penny roll had to do for Tuesday.

At Colepeter's coffee shop, the tables were in places like pews in church, with seats each side and each seat held four persons, or six if the shop was busy. It was very respectable and select at Colepeter's. Although things were so cheap, they would serve only nice people. You could get a cup of coffee with plenty of sugar in it for a penny, and they didn't say anything if you took with you a penny roll or a saveloy to eat there, so long as they didn't see them. Once I got halfway through a saveloy and had the misfortune to drop it and it rolled right into the gangway between the pews and laid there until Miss Clara, the waitress, came with a dustpan and swept it up. She looked round first to see if anyone claimed it, but no one did, and I kept my eyes on a newspaper. I was sorry because it was a decent saveloy, but I was more careful after that.

Although they served poor customers like me, they catered for rich people as well. Some customers had good dinners every day that cost as much as one and six, but their tables had tablecloths on. Now I've started talking about Colepeter's, I may as well tell you about that coffee shop and not leave it till later on as I meant to do at the first. All the time I worked in Rye Lane I went to that shop for dinner and tea. They didn't open on Sunday, but that didn't trouble me much. I didn't get up early that day, or if I did I'd lie down again after breakfast and read Scott. I liked reading about how the Earl of Leicester entertained Queen Elizabeth in *Kenilworth*, and the big feast they had, such a lot of food, enough to make anyone sick, but I shouldn't have minded risking that for once. I expect all that food made them livery and disagreeable and that's why they always carried a sword.

The main thing that kept Colepeter's select was that they wouldn't serve bloaters. If you could afford it, you could have an egg for a penny or a nice-looking rasher of bacon for tuppence, but bloaters – no. It was like the barber in *Nicholas Nickleby* who wouldn't shave a coal-heaver and said he drew the line at bakers! So Colepeter's drew the line at bloaters. A stranger who didn't know this rule would come in and order 'A pint of "corfee", two "doorsteps" and a bloater,' and Miss Clara would sniff and say, 'We don't keep fish,' and the man would go away growling. Some would get a bit saucy and say, 'I shouldn't think you would *keep* it, if you got any sense,' but Miss Clara, who was very dignified and nice-mannered, never answered them back. She just turned away and sniffed.

The best thing of all was Colepeters's steak puddings. They were boiled in little basins and then turned out on a plate and brought to you hot and steaming. Sometimes a newcomer who wanted one would order 'A baby's head,' but they didn't do it twice, not after the look Miss Clara gave them. After you had a good sniff at the steam, you put your knife in at the top and as you cut it down a lot of rich gravy came out.

If Mrs Todgers in *Martin Chuzzlewit* had given her commercial gentlemen puddings like those, they wouldn't have worried her like they did about not getting enough gravy.

Quite a lot of the customers were regulars and came from Tilling's omnibus stables near by. I liked to listen to their talk about horses. They were too hungry at dinner time to talk much, but at tea time, although they only had half an hour, they would argue and talk all the time, mostly about Gladstone and Disraeli and what they'd like to do to the Irish members who were obstructing things in Parliament. If they said anything a bit strong Miss Clara would come out from the back and tell them about it. She was very particular about language, and it got to be a bit of a joke with some of the cheeky customers. Perhaps one of them would be telling the others a funny tale and just as he was coming to the funniest part at the end he'd wait a bit until Miss Clara came near to serve somebody, and then the others would say, 'Hush ... hush ... here comes Miss Clara' in a loud whisper. The joke was usually quite harmless – they only did it to tease her because she always looked shocked and sniffed.

One big red-faced man who was a commercial traveller used to come every Friday and have a big tea. He enjoyed saying things to shock Miss Clara. I think he must have laid awake at night thinking them out. Once he said something so funny just when I was drinking my tea, and I nearly choked laughing and some of the tea spouted out of my nose. It didn't matter much as there wasn't any table cloth, but I kept one eye out for Miss Clara. This man was fat and jolly-looking like Falstaff in Shakespeare, and he'd got a nose like Bardolph. He didn't drink a lot of tea but he ate plenty of buttered toast and always got all shiny. He didn't keep his jokes for the people who sat near him, but spoke loud enough for all the shop to hear, and smiled round at everybody all the time. He even looked at me once and smiled, so I got to look forward to his coming. It didn't matter what anyone said to him, he'd always got a funny answer. Once a customer said, as he came in and sat down at his table, 'Good evening, Mr Catterpole, how are you?' Mr Catterpole put on a sad sort of look and said mournfully, 'I am well, I thank you, but weary and sick at heart.' Then the other said, 'I'm sorry to hear that, Mr Catterpole. What's the trouble, if I may ask?' and he replied, 'Well, I've been away since Monday, working hard travelling about, and now just as I thought I'd have a nice restful weekend I find that both my wives have got the mumps. So inconsiderate of them. Don't you think so, Miss Clara?' Once he said a rude word right out before everybody. He was telling us all about a time when he put up for the night at a country inn, and when he went to bed he found that a new servant had left the warming pan in his bed. He never noticed it at first, but got into bed sharp and sat on it. He said, 'I did feel an ass — I jumped out pretty quick and rang the bell, and when the girl came I said, "What do you mean by leaving the warming pan in my bed?" And she said, "Well, zur, you said you warnted yer bed waarmed, didn't you?" and I said, "Yes, but I didn't say I wanted my bum warmed, did I?" ' Miss Clara came running out and said, 'Better language, please!' Then he looked at us all as if he was astonished and said, 'Language? Gentlemen, I appeal to you.' Then he burst out laughing and we all laughed and Miss Clara went back looking like one of Foxe's Martyrs, sniffing louder than ever.

One evening when I was having my tea, I got talking to a young man who told me that he had come up from Ely with horses for the bus company, and had found his way to

Colepeter's to have some tea. I thought of that little brown girl that I used to look at in church when I was at the college in Reading, and who came from Ely in Cambridgeshire. I asked him if his Ely was the same, and he said it was. So then I asked him if he knew anyone named Tingey down his way. He said there were a lot of people with that name in a village near Ely. Some of them bred trotting horses and did a lot of business that way, and one of the Tingeys lived in the largest house in the place and was called Squire Tom, but some of the others were not so well off. I asked him if he knew a little girl there whose name was Fanny 'Topknot', and he asked, 'What sort of a girl?' I told him that she had nice crinkly brown hair and was very pretty to look at, but he couldn't remember that one. He said that all Cambridgeshire 'gells' were pretty. He wanted to know where I'd met her, so I told him about her coming to that college on a visit about five years ago. We figured out that she'd be grown to a big girl now and he promised to find out if she lived there and let me know next time he came up with horses. But though I looked for him for a long time after that, I never saw him again. I wished I had been born in Cambridgeshire instead of London, and kept thinking about that nice little girl and I wished that I was rich and able to go down to Ely to look for her. I wondered whether I should know her now that she was bigger. I didn't suppose she'd know me, nor look at me, me being only an errand boy, but I should like to see her again. Somehow, I'd never forgotten her. I thought I was a fool not to have asked that young chap the name of the village near Ely.

Now I will go on to tell you how I got on at Mr Kenelly's boot shop. I had to get there at eight and take down the shutters, sweep the shop and then do dusting and take out and deliver parcels of boots to all parts of Peckham and Camberwell. When I got used to the smell of leather and learnt how to brush up all the hundreds of pairs of boots that hung all around the walls of the shop, all of which had to be brushed up once a week, and when I was allowed to help to serve the customers at busy times, I thought that the boot and shoe trade was a good one to be in. Everybody wanted boots or shoes and there wasn't any society like the Good Templars to persuade people to go about bare-footed, so I felt pretty safe and tried to learn all I could about boots.

I had to take out the parcels in a large blue bag which I slung over my shoulder. Sometimes I had to take a whole lot of ladies' boots loose in the bag for a customer to choose and try on at her own house. I often waited a long time on the doorstep, but now and then a kind young servant would let me sit in the kitchen and would talk to me while she was getting on with the potatoes or something. One of them asked me where I went on Sunday evenings, if I went to church. I said that I was a Christadelphian and she said, 'What's that?' So I told her what they used to preach about in Swansea, about the Millennium and Armageddon, and the End of the World coming soon, and about the awful pictures they stuck up every Sunday. She said she wouldn't like to attend that church, it would give her the creeps. She'd rather go to the Nunhead Cemetery on Sunday night – it wasn't so bad there, lots of flowers and a seat here and there where you could rest nice and quiet and not many people about. Then she gave me a pair of her shoes to be heeled and said that we ought not to charge much because they were such a tiny size. She said that her missus wished she had such small feet, and would I please bring them back next Saturday as her evening out was on Sunday. By this time, the lady had made up her mind and selected a pair to suit her, and back I went with my load. Mr Kenelly never grumbled about me being so long on those errands. I expect he knew what those ladies were like and what a time it took them to make up their minds.

Being out in the fresh air so much made me hungry, but I never bought anything to eat between meals. I kept telling myself that if I did I wouldn't enjoy my dinner so much. The hours at Mr Kenelly's weren't so bad. We shut at nine except on Friday and Saturday when we were quite late in closing.

I used to wonder why the shops in London didn't have a half holiday in the middle of the week like they did in Swansea, and I thought that London was behind-hand and not so wonderful after all. When you work for seventy-four hours from Monday morning to Saturday night, and don't leave off until it's nearly time to go to bed, you do get tired of it and wish you had a half holiday once a week like workmen and office people do.

Once when I went to the grocer's to get things for Mrs Kenelly, the young men there were talking about the long hours and I thought I would tell them about the shops in Swansea and how early they closed. They were astonished. They said that they had an evening off about once in two months if they asked nicely for it, but if you wanted one oftener you might get the sack because you thought more of pleasure than business.

I hadn't been at Mr Kenelly's long before I got a new lodger for Mrs Pagles. I went in every new shop that was opening in Peckham and asked if anyone there wanted a nice bedroom, and a young man from a tailor's came and paid Mrs Pagles four shillings a week for the big bedroom. My little landlady was pleased about it and reduced my rent to two shillings and sixpence a week and gave me a cup of cocoa. So I didn't mind working till eleven on Saturdays because Mr Kenelly used to send me into the back room at ten o'clock and his wife gave me a cup of coffee and some bread and cheese. So that was another little extra and I thought it was kind of them. I liked helping to serve customers on Saturday nights, especially when they were young ladies who wanted button-up boots. You had to go down on one knee and cock their leg up on your other one, then pull the boot on and take a button hook and button 'em up. Some of the fashionable boots went halfway up their leg. But it wasn't so easy when some of them wanted boots with elastic sides. It was a bit of a pull to get them on especially when the lady was rather old and fat and had legs the same thickness all the way down. I couldn't get the

96

elastic sides to stretch far enough and sometimes pulled the tags off. But in spite of that they would have springside boots and didn't believe in the new fangled button-up sort. Men were much easier to serve. They pulled the boots on themselves and didn't take long to make up their minds. One man whose boots hurt him left them with me after he had bought a comfortable pair and told me to chuck them away. They were hardly worn at all and only about two sizes larger than those I wore, so I showed them to Mr Kenelly and he said I could have them. That was another extra and I got my pennorth out of them.

But in spite of these little helps it was a job to make eight shillings do and I often went hungry at the end of the week. Sometimes I wished I could meet someone like the Artful Dodger and get taken home by him like Oliver Twist was. Those boys seemed to have had an easy time. Old Fagin wasn't such a bad sort. There was a big fire in his room and he fried plenty of sausages for those boys and gave them gin and water. It made me hungry to read about it. I had never had as many sausages as I could eat.

My clothes got worn and shabby too, and however I should be able to buy a new pair of trousers I couldn't think. I don't know what would have happened if I hadn't found a way to earn a little more. I noticed that some of the shops in Rye Lane didn't have enough work to employ a boy all day, so they used to get a boy for a few shillings a week to take down the shutters in the morning, sweep out the shop and now and then give the windows a rub-over, and then come at night and put the shutters up. I thought I would try for a job like that, so I went in all those shops and asked if they would think of me if their boy left, and soon after I got engaged at a toy and fancy goods shop. It was kept by two ladies and it had been a china and glass shop but the man who had it went broke. They paid me three shillings a week and I went there half an hour before I was due at the boot shop. There were ten shutters to take down and carry round the back, and that and the sweeping out didn't take long — I was done easily

ore eight, and after I shut up Mr Kenelly's shop I went to
.ie toy shop and put their shutters up. It was a bit of luck
getting a job like that — it meant a good dinner every day —
and when soon after I got another job of the same sort I
thought that my luck was properly in. I had heard that the
boy who did the jeweller's shop was leaving so I made a
bargain with him. If he'd speak for me and I got taken on I'd
give him two shillings. So he did, and I got their work as well.

I got Mr Pagles to give me a knock soon after six and that
gave me plenty of time to wash and get breakfast before I
went to open the jeweller's at seven. There were a lot more
shutters to that shop and they were heavy, being lined with
sheet-iron because of the valuable goods they kept. There was
more work there than at the toy shop. I had to go in my tea
half hour to put up the outside gas lamps ready for lighting
up. They had to be taken down at shutting up time and put
away. But they paid me four shillings a week and didn't mind
waiting until I'd closed the other two shops before I closed
theirs. So then I had fifteen shillings a week coming in and
felt quite happy. I soon saved enough to get another pair of
trousers.

I thought a good deal then about saving some money,
whether it was wiser to save some or just spend it as it came
in. If I wanted a shop of my own some day I shouldn't be
able to get one unless I saved, one couldn't get a shop
without money — all those people who kept shops must have
saved money to buy them. Mr Kenelly must have saved to get
his business — he seemed to be doing well and had plenty to
eat after paying rent and wages and things. Once he sent me
for a whole peck of peas for dinner. Of course if you were
too poor to save anything, when you got old or out of work
you had to go in the workhouse unless your children helped
you, and that wasn't safe to rely on. They'd have enough to
do to look after themselves. Again, if people didn't make and
save such a lot of money like rich people do, many poor
people might have had more of it paid to them in wages —
and if *they* saved some of it there might not be any work-

house wanted. On the other hand if everyone saved all they could and didn't spend much there wouldn't be so many shops wanted. It was all very puzzling. I wished I had someone to explain it all to me. I wanted to do what was right and 'take no heed of the morrow'. At the same time, if I didn't look after myself no one else would. So I finished up by putting five shillings in the Post Office Savings.

Two ladies managed the jeweller's shop and a very old gentleman did the watch and clock repairs. He used to come to the door to let me in at seven every morning, but he seldom spoke to me. But the ladies did when I went in during my dinner hour every month to clean the glass showcases.

The ladies were very educated and spoke nicely. They said once that it would be good for me and respectable if I went to their church on Sundays. I told them that I was rather tired on Sunday and laid in bed late, but I might go in the evening. I said 'perhaps'. They asked me many questions too but I never told them much except about Wales. When I told them that, they started whispering to each other and I could see that one of them was egging the other on to say something. So at last she asked me if it was true that young people in Wales did their courting in bed. I told them that I had never heard of such a thing — neither had I — but I don't think they believed me.

As I had to go to these two shops and do things for them in meal times I had to cut down the time I spent at Colepeter's and it was a bit of a rush to get back to the boot shop in time. Some days when I had to go out about eleven o'clock with a parcel of boots to be delivered at a place a long way off, I would run all the way there and back and so get time to have a bit of dinner before my usual dinner hour came. Then I could spend that hour doing things at my two extra shops. I got fourpence from the jeweller's for doing the glass cases.

The ladies at the toy shop didn't talk much to me. They seemed rather miserable and grumpy. I don't think they did much business. They didn't trouble much about dressing the window and it looked to me that they might soon go broke like the china shop man did before them. But the poor ladies paid me my three shillings every week and I did my best to keep the outside of the shop and the window clean.

After things had gone on like this for about six months Mr Kenelly told me that he had sold his business to a company. I was sorry to hear that. They had been so kind to me. He was sorry too in a way, but said he'd had such a good offer that he couldn't refuse it, but that I needn't worry, the new people would be sure to keep me on.

Soon after, two gentlemen came to value the stock and one of them who was the head of the firm asked me what wages I was getting. When I told him eight shillings and that Mr Kenelly had promised me a rise soon, he said he could get any amount of boys in Woolwich for five shillings a week. But after Mr and Mrs Kenelly had spoken to him he told me that I could stay on at the same money. I think he meant that all the time, because I saw him laughing afterwards when he was talking to Mrs Kenelly. (He was a nice man really, because some time after when he came as usual on Monday morning to inspect the shop and talk to the manager, he watched me brushing up the boots and then came over and put two shillings in my hand.)

At the end of the week Mr Kenelly moved out and a manager and his wife came to live over the shop. His furniture came at the same time as Mr Kenelly's was being taken out, so there was rather a confusion and I never had a chance to say good-bye to them, and I wondered whether Mrs Kenelly had told the new people about that bit of supper I got on Saturday nights.

I laid awake a bit that night thinking about it. So on Friday when the manager's wife sent me out for grocery, I took them into the back room and asked her if I could chop some fire wood or carry some coals up to the sitting room like I used to for Mrs Kenelly. When I'd done that she asked me things about the lady. Whether she was nice looking. And did she dress up much, and if she went in the shop to serve. I told her that Mrs Kenelly didn't trouble much about dress and seldom came in the shop, but she used to talk very kindly to me when she gave me my supper on Saturday night. I said she made nice coffee.

On Saturday the new lady gave me a nice supper of cold rabbit and pork as well as a small glass of beer. And I had something good every Saturday after that.

There was much more work at that shop after Mr Kenelly left. The new people had a better shop front put in with large sheets of brass nearly down to the pavement. This had to be cleaned every morning with acid, and it was a long job particularly at the corners because of dogs. I began to notice the brasses on other shops and tried to get mine as bright as those; but I couldn't manage it. I think new brass doesn't polish up so easily as older brass does. Anyhow, it made the shop look better, we did more business and I had more parcels to deliver.

While I was cleaning that brass one morning I remembered that doctor at the zoo who had treated me so kindly and what he said about his brass plate. So that gave me an idea. A doctor up Rye Lane had two brass plates, one on the garden wall and one on the gate, and they looked as if they hadn't been cleaned for years, they had gone nearly brown. So one day in my dinner hour I took some brass rags in my pocket and borrowed a little of the acid which I put in a medicine bottle and went and cleaned both those plates. It took a long time but they were quite bright when I'd done. Then I knocked on the door and a very old servant came. She said the doctor was out and what was the matter with me and if I wanted to see the doctor I must come after six. I didn't go up that way with boots that evening, but next night I did and saw the doctor. He said, 'Well, what's the trouble?' Then I told him what I had done and do you know? He had to go outside to see if it was true. He'd been in and out both those days and hadn't noticed the difference. He was a dreamy sort of doctor and couldn't have been very sharp. But he seemed pleased and gave me threepence. I thanked him and said that for threepence a week I would keep his brass plates always bright and his door knocker as well. He shut his eyes and thought about it for a bit and then said that he would agree to that but he couldn't be bothered to pay it every week, he would pay me a shilling on the first of every month. So I said, 'Yes sir, that'll suit me, thank you,' because I thought it would be better to have a whole shilling to put in the Post Office instead of having to save up the threepences and perhaps spend some of it. It wasn't much trouble to keep those plates clean and shiny. I kept a brass rag in my pocket and gave them a rub every time I went past with parcels. But I had some trouble with other boys who would keep smearing their dirty and greasy fingers over the brass. Nearly every time I went by I found them smeared.

It was a long time before I caught one doing it and when he saw me coming he ran away. I chased him up Rye Lane and caught him outside a shop but before I did much to him he fell backwards and broke the glass in a shop doorway. We both went away then and for a long time I didn't walk on that side of the street.

The first of the month seemed a long time coming and then I remembered that there were more than four weeks in most months. So I worked it out and found that I should lose four threepences in a year. So that doctor wasn't so dreamy after all.

I wasn't surprised when one day the ladies at the toy shop told me that they had sold their business. They didn't give me any notice to leave off coming to open and shut so I took it that they were going to pass me over with the fixtures. If they had not done this, I might have stuck to the boot trade and perhaps after years got to be a manager, and then after years and years I might have saved enough money to get a boot shop of my own. It was the sale of that toy shop that altered all that.

Mr Gaynibb who bought the toy and fancy business was a short, stout man with a large red beard that grew like a thick fringe round his face, so that he never had to wear a necktie.

102

He told me some time later that he had started business in the New Cut, Lambeth, when he was a boy, by selling things from a barrow, by shouting out and saying funny things to get a crowd round. After that he took a shop and carried on in the same way and did so well that by the time he was forty he had made a fortune and was able to retire from business. But after a time he got tired of idleness so he took a public house where he lost a lot of money. So he got out of that and retired again, but he found that having nothing to do gave him the 'perishing hump'. So when he heard of this business going he bought it to amuse himself and have something to do. When he took over the place they didn't take stock of the toys and things, he just looked them over and then made an offer for the lot as they stood. And he got the lot cheap.

He was rather 'rough and ready' but very straightforward and honest — except to his wife — and I wondered whether the customers would take to him. They were rather different from the New Cut shoppers — you had to call them Madam.

When he'd been there a week he asked me to come in and see him dinner time. So I went and found that he wanted me to leave the boot shop and come and work for him only. He asked me what wages I was getting there, so I told him eight shillings and what with his shop and the jeweller's I was getting fifteen shillings a week. He said it wasn't much for all that work and said, 'What about chucking those jobs up and come and work for me? I'll give you thirteen bob a week and if we get on together I'll soon give you more.' I thanked him very much and said I would think it over and let him know next day. So I did think it over — nearly all night. ('If I accepted his offer I should have two shillings a week less coming in — but he looked a kind old chap — it was rather good of him to offer thirteen shillings a week just for the work of one shop — and yet he'd promised to raise the wages soon. If I didn't have to work at three shops every day, I wouldn't get all tired out like I was every night. I could lay in bed an hour more in the morning. Yes, and get done earlier at night not having the two other shops to see to after I'd closed. Yes, but what about that nice supper the boot manager's wife gave me every Saturday? And those two ladies at the jeweller's who weren't too proud to talk to me like they did. I'd miss them. Was the toy trade as good as boots? Oh! Cuss it. What had I better do? But that old chap said he'd pay me more soon. If I worked hard for him he might make it up to the fifteen shillings. The toy trade must be good if he could afford to pay all that just for a shop boy — and the boot shop could only pay eight — Oh! Blow — I know what I'll do, I'll ask the boot manager if the company will pay me more, and I'll tell him about the good offer I have had.')

Next morning I spoke to the manager about it and he said the firm only allowed him so much for the shop boy but if I stayed on I might after a time get put in some other branch and get fifteen shillings a week as a junior assistant and if I was lucky I might later on be made manager and start at thirty shillings a week and perhaps get the rooms over the shop to live in. I was silly to leave a good trade like boots and go into a trade with no prospects, and if I would stay on he'd give me two shillings a week more out of his own pocket. I shouldn't have felt comfortable if I'd let him do that, so I gave notice to leave.

At dinner time I told the ladies at the jeweller's that I should leave off coming to their shop in a week's time. And they asked me to come in after closing time and talk it over.

When I went in their husbands were there; I hadn't spoken to those gentlemen before. They went off every day to a shop in the West End. They didn't say much that night but let the ladies do all the talking. They would be sorry if I left and if I'd come and work for them entirely they would teach me the trade and pay me ten shillings a week. The old gentleman would show me how to repair clocks, watches and jewellery, so that I could take his place later on. 'Think it over, Tom. It's a gentleman's trade and no boy ever started in it on such good terms. When you are older you might get a position as jeweller's salesman and get as much as four pounds a week. Tell your parents Tom. I'm sure they will agree.'

I thought it was a very kind offer and thanked them and then I told them the truth about things. I had never told any of those I worked for in Rye Lane that I hadn't a good home to go to and was all alone, and had to keep myself on what I earned. I never told them where I lodged or anything but led them to believe that I had a home like other boys. I was afraid that if they knew they might get rid of me in case I stole something, although I would never do that. No doubt I could have managed on the ten shillings the jewellers offered but I wouldn't be able to buy clothes — not even the second-hand things I was wearing then. One would want to wear smarter and more expensive things in a shop like that.

So I told the ladies all about it and they were astonished when I said that I had once kept myself and paid rent on eight shillings a week. I told them that I would always remember their kindness and perhaps now I would be able to go to their church on Sunday morning.

I felt happy all the rest of the week looking forward to an easier time and wondering how I should get on in the toy and fancy goods trade.

10

Mr Gaynibb hadn't known about the doctor's brass plates so I didn't give that job up but did it now and then in my dinner hour. My first work at the toy shop was to empty the glass cases behind the counter of the fancy goods, sort them out and polish them up. There were heaps of things besides toys in that shop: purses, ladies' bags, prayer and hymn books, cigar cases, pocketbooks, little china ornaments and many other useless things that people buy to give as presents. Many of those were soiled and shabby and Mr Gaynibb said he would sell them off very cheap and get shut of them. 'Never keep a lot of dead stock hanging about.'

Very few customers came in, but he didn't seem to mind. He kept walking about the shop with his hands in his pockets, stopping every now and then to see what I was doing and examining the latest fancy thing that I had dug out of the cases. He had a fine grey parrot in a cage at the end of the shop. Every now and then he'd go near and whistle to it and the bird whistled back.

It was an amusing parrot. He said it could talk and whistle part of a tune out of an opera. At eleven o'clock he gave me a small bottle and told me to go and get him threepenn'orth of rum and when I got back I was to keep it in my pocket until he asked me for it. I believe he did this so that his wife shouldn't know. She came into the shop once or twice and talked to the parrot. A large black cat came in with her; it stared at the parrot and kept wagging its tail. I don't think they could have liked each other much because when that bird saw the cat it got excited and climbed all over the cage and said, 'Sheederblack-Sheederblack', quite plainly. I couldn't make out what it meant but I was amused because I remembered selling some 'talking' parrots once, but this was the first one I'd heard say anything.

I had to go out for rum three times that day and I wondered why he didn't buy a big bottle at a time and have done with it, but afterwards I saw that it was because he didn't want his wife to know. He could keep the small bottle in his pocket: but if he had a large one she would see it when she got poking about behind the counter like she did.

While I worked for him he sent me for rum so many times that the lining of my jacket pocket got worn right through by carrying that little bottle. The more rum he had the more he talked to me and the parrot. He told me lots of things about his shop in the New Cut and the fortune he made there, and about the pub where he dropped a lot of it. It seemed to me that he'd engaged me partly to have someone to talk to and run private errands.

He was a very sociable old chap except with the customers. If they were finicky he soon lost patience and told them to take their custom somewhere else. I soon saw that if he went on like that there wouldn't be much trade left, so I tried to make up for it by being extra nice to the customers I served. I soon got to know what would happen when Mr Gaynibb was serving a lady who wanted a present for a gentleman, but didn't know what to select for him. He'd get out pocket-books, notebooks, cigar cases and a lot of similar things and tell her the prices of each of the things over and over again because she'd keep forgetting. Then after she'd done a lot of fiddling about with the things his face would begin to get red and he'd start humming some tune. I knew it was a sure sign when he began to hum — it was like a kettle simmering just before the water boils. Then if the lady said, 'I think I'll leave it — it's not for me — I'll get him to come himself,' then the kettle boiled right over. He'd slam all the things back into the cases and yell out, 'Oh, you will, will you? Well, if he's like you, you can tell him to "B" well keep away.' The customer would go out quite frightened and he had to have another drop of rum.

Sometimes he'd get quite annoyed if a customer came in just as he was telling me something funny that happened in the New Cut. Of course, he couldn't have gone on like that if he hadn't been independent and rich. At the same time I think he was sorry that he lost his temper so often. He would try to excuse it by saying that it did the customers good to be 'told off' now and then. He said that they got too stuck up through tradesmen kow-towing to them and being 'much obliged' and all that, and that it made them think they were patronising the shopkeeper when they bought anything.

On Friday in my first week, Mrs Gaynibb went off for the day to visit her sister. She left instructions about 'the Guv'nor's dinner'. There was a plate of cold meat in the back room and he was to warm up some potatoes. He said, 'Yes, dear.' But just before one o'clock he asked me if I knew of any good dining rooms near. I told him of Colepeter's and what a good trade they did. He asked if they sent out dinners and I said I thought so. I'd seen the girl who helped in the kitchen go out with a tray with a white cloth over it. Then he said I was to go and order two dinners to be sent. He didn't quite know what he'd have, whether beef or mutton. I told him about the beef-steak puddings and how nice and juicy they were, but when he heard they were only fourpence each he said, 'No. Just you go and ask them to send two dinners of anything they've got that's nice.' I felt very important going to Colepeter's with an order like that and Miss Clara didn't sniff at all. She said, 'Thank you. It shall have immediate attention.' I asked her about 'what she'd got that's nice', and she said that everything was nice today, but she could recommend the roast pork with stuffing and baked potatoes with brussels sprouts and apple sauce, and apple pie to follow. That sounded nice to me, so I ordered two lots.

When I got back he said I wasn't to go off to dinner as

usual but have one of the dinners in the shop while he had his in the back parlour. When the dinners came he said they smelt jolly nice and he told me to give the cold meat to the cat and put the potatoes in the dustbin but be sure to cover them up with the tea leaves and other stuff that was there. I had a better dinner that day than I'd had for years and years.

I was glad to find that his wife went off every Friday after that, and each time he sent me to Colepeter's to order two lots of 'anything they'd got that's nice'.

When he paid me on Saturday, he said he would give me a shilling rise next week — and he did this four weeks running until my wages were seventeen shillings a week, and then he stopped. I saved some more money this way. I had taken my Sunday suit for every day use a long time before this, but now I could afford to look a bit smarter on Sunday, so I saved up and bought a long light overcoat called a 'duster' for fifteen shillings. It came a good way down so that the shabby things underneath didn't show much. With a bowler hat that cost two shillings and sixpence I fancy I was as smart as any of them when I went for a walk up the Rye on Sundays.

One day when I was tired of having so little work to do, I asked Mr Gaynibb if he'd let me try to dress the window and make some fresh tickets. He had done some tickets with 'Oh! Mother, Look!' on them, like he used to do in the New Cut. I never said anything but I didn't think they were quite the thing — not in a classy place like Peckham. When he saw the tickets I had done, he sent me for a lot of cards and some ticket ink and got me to make tickets for nearly everything in the shop. We put baskets filled with very cheap things in the wide doorway and sold a lot of the old stock from there. I had to stand a little way back in the shop and be ready to pounce out and try to sell something if anyone stopped and looked interested. It was a spider sort of a job. I had to watch out too to see that nothing was stolen. One afternoon I went to sleep standing there, but that was after one of those Friday dinners.

There was a very long sideboard counter which stood against the wall and ran the whole length of the shop from the doorway. The top of it was covered with toys and boxes of stock, and the front was hidden by large things like children's wooden horses and hoops. I used to move the things and dust a bit at a time, but on one rainy morning I moved everything so as to give the sideboard a good wash down. The top looked all the better for a clean up, but when I started on the front I found that the panels moved sideways. They were hard to move, being so clogged up with dirt, but I got one open and looked inside. I found that it was chock-full of glass tumblers. It was the same when I moved the other panels. There were hundreds and hundreds of glasses all crusted with dirt and covered with spider's webs. So I went to the back parlour and told Mr Gaynibb. He seemed astonished and said, 'Tumblers? What tumblers? Where did you say?' When he came out and saw them, he opened his eyes pretty wide and then thought for a bit. Then he said, 'Oh, yes, of course. Tumblers. Yes, I remember now.'

I didn't believe he'd known anything about them. He was just letting on at me that he did. I expect those glasses had been packed away and forgotten when the place was a china shop, so it's no wonder they went broke. Mr Gaynibb said he would make a splash and sell 'em all off at a penny each, so I had to get out a dozen or so and wash them. Well, do you know, I found that those glasses were best cut glass and a very pretty pattern. I thought I would tell Mr Gaynibb that I'd been in the china and glass trade and that tumblers of that quality were sold in Wales at eightpence each. He had a good look at them and thought for a bit, then he said that he'd be ninety years old before he sold the last of them if he charged eightpence, but he thought he'd try to get more than a penny so we'd better mark them up at tuppence ha'penny each or two for fourpence ha'penny. I had to get a large card and make a ticket. He made me put, 'Oh! Mother, Look!' on it, but the rest I put in myself after thinking for some time.

I washed and polished up a lot more of the things and then we filled the baskets at the door with them and put the big ticket on top. Many people stopped to look, but we only sold five that day in spite of that nice ticket I'd made.

OH! MOTHER, LOOK!
GENUINE
SOPRAFINO
CUT-GLASS TUMBLERS
2$\frac{1}{2}$d EACH   OR 2 FOR 4$\frac{1}{2}$d

Next day we only sold three and then Mr Gaynibb began to swear. He said we ought to mark them up a penny each as he'd said. But we did better on Thursday, and people who had bought one before came back for more. Some of them bought six and they must have told their friends as we sold over fifty that day. On Friday we were so busy that he had to come in the doorway and help me dish them out. He got quite excited and started shouting out a lot of patter like he must have done in the New Cut. Then I shouted out too and such a lot of people came crowding round. After a while the cheesemonger next door came in and complained about it because somebody had pinched a hock of bacon off his board outside. He must have been a religious sort of man because he went away looking very shocked because of the things Mr Gaynibb said to him and about going to hell.

We had a bigger crowd than ever on Saturday, through us shouting, and then a policeman came and said we'd have to stop it. So then we left off hollering and left the ticket to do the work, and I made a big show of the glasses in the window with another big ticket on. I expect Christmas being so near had something to do with it, because we kept on selling more and more.

There seemed to be no end to those tumblers and I had

plenty to do what with washing, polishing and wrapping them up. Mr Gaynibb was very happy, being busy like that. Many people bought toys as well as the glasses and if little children came with them he was so kind and patient with them, showing them all different toys for the little things to choose from, and he never boiled over once.

If nobody happened to be in the shop he walked up and down whistling and singing bits out of comic songs to the parrot and trying to teach it swear words. He tried to get it to repeat two lines from some song:

> She had a black and a roving eye,
> And her name was Maritana.

He said that over and over again and the bird listened with its head on one side and its eyes closed. Then by and by when all was quiet it would scream out, 'She'd der black — she'd a black.' That's as far as it got in that song, but it could say many other words. Mr Gaynibb told me that he'd got it from the pub he used to keep. That place was 'a house of call' for 'snobs', meaning bootmakers, and customers had taught the bird to say things that it shouldn't. When they wanted to tease a bootmaker, they said, 'Wax' because of the cobblers' wax they used. So when the parrot felt like it, it would rattle off a lot of words and whistle a tune out of *The Bohemian Girl*, but it always finished up by saying in a deep voice, 'Wax, you ——, wax!' If a lady happened to be in the shop when it did this she would look rather startled, but I don't think we lost any custom through it because sometimes the ladies would come again and bring a friend, and after buying some little thing would ask me to get the parrot to whistle that pretty song again. It generally did if I whistled a bit first, and then it went on saying things, but it always finished up with the shoe-maker's insult, and the ladies would go away looking pleased.

We sold all those tumblers in three weeks and then Mr Gaynibb had more time to talk to me and tell me again how he'd made his fortune. He was kind enough to say that he wished he'd had a chap like me working for him when he was in the New Cut selling job lines. He told me how to go about it if ever I wanted to make a fortune in the same way, and the names of the firms that sold soiled goods, samples and throw-outs, and he advised me to get a shop in a cheap working-class neighbourhood. 'You can make more money out of those sort of people than you can out of the stuck-up lot about here,' he said. 'And don't forget money is hard to get, but it's a damn sight harder to hold.' He had other sayings: 'You save it in bits and it goes in dollops', 'Everybody tries to get it out of you and do you down', 'Friends will borrow it of you, or advise you to buy shares in companies that you know nothing about, or get you to buy some rotten pub like I did, and when you're on the rocks, they'll laugh. It's like that song George Leybourne used to sing —

> When you've got the money, you're a brick, brick,
>   brick.
> When you've got the money, all your pals will
>   stick.
> But when you've got no money,
> The world has lost its honey,
> And you'll find you're up a pole, when you ask for
>   tick, tick, tick.

'That's quite true, and don't you forget it. And now go and get me threepenn'orth of rum.'

Many people came in on Christmas Eve for some of those 'soprafino' tumblers, but we had sold them all, and as many kept coming and asking for those and nothing else, he got impatient and the kettle boiled over several times.

I was left all alone in my lodgings on Christmas Day as Mr and Mrs Pagles went off early to spend Christmas and Boxing Day with a brother in Bermondsey, and the other lodger had gone goodness knows where. When they'd gone, I went all over the cottage looking in the bedrooms. Everything was very neat and clean but the furniture wasn't up to much and on all the mantelpieces they had little old clocks that wouldn't go and had been saved for ornament. I looked in the cupboard in the kitchen where the cocoa and marmalade was kept, and had a spoonful of condensed milk out of a tin that was there, and I borrowed a little of the marmalade for my breakfast. Then I went out for a walk. It was quite sunny out, not like Christmas at all, only a bit cold.

There were a good many people about, some with books going to church and lots of others hurrying along and looking happy. I met whole families of them now and then, mother looking worried carrying a baby and father behind holding two other children's hands and a little bigger girl carrying a new doll. I expect they were all off to spend Christmas with grandpa and granny. They all looked pleased except mother and the baby. Then I went up Rye Lane and met 'Uncle'. He was a fat old gentleman and was going along slowly and carrying a large jar and puffing. He stopped me and said would I like to earn fourpence? He'd give me that if I'd carry the jar for him. It was full of whisky and I'd have to be careful not to drop it. 'Only to the top of the Rye, to Nunhead Grove.' I said yes I would, rather. That jar was heavy — it must have had a gallon in it, and I had to keep changing hands. I think he must have had some of it before he started; he was rather jolly and talked and joked with me all the way. He said he was going to spend Christmas with his married niece and her family and there'd be a lot of other brothers and sisters-in-law there. He went there every year, and they always said that it wouldn't be Christmas unless they had Uncle there. Then he tried over bits of a new song he was going to sing. When we got to the corner of the road he gave me the money and took the jar. He didn't want them to think that he hadn't carried it himself. He said, 'You ought to see their faces when they come to the door — they'll be all over me. They're always pleased to see Uncle.' I thought so too — him and that jar.

Then I went up One Tree Hill and had a view right over

London, with the sun shining on St Paul's, and then I began to get hungry. Colepeter's was closed and I had to go a long way before I found a coffee shop open, but they hadn't got any dinner ready, so I had a bloater. I stopped there in the warm as long as I could, looking at the *Graphic* and other papers, and then walked home. I made a nice fire with some wood I found and some coals that I took from the back of the heap, and had some bread and marmalade for tea. I sat reading *Woodstock* until I got sick of it.

It was very cold and rather foggy that night when I went out again. The streets were dark and deserted, but most of the parlour windows of small houses were lighted up and it was quite fun to stand for a time outside a house and listen to the songs they were singing inside and the thumping on the piano. At some of the houses you could hear screams of laughter and choruses of comic songs. Everybody seemed to be having a merry time. There was hardly a soul about those streets and I wondered how many of the six million people in London were wandering about lonely with no money and perhaps no homes. It didn't affect me because I'd got plenty of money and a nice room to go to and perhaps it was better for me to be out in the fresh air instead of being stuck in a stuffy parlour with a lot of other people until late at night, talking, laughing and singing and very likely drinking too much beer.

Going along like that, I found myself in the Old Kent Road and it looked as mouldy as ever there. I found a baked potato man at one corner, so I bought a couple and stopped to have a talk with him, but he was grumpy and disagreeable. He said that there was no bleeding trade about and he hadn't taken in enough to pay for the coke he was burning.

I went back home with a hot potato in each trouser pocket, and I found some salt and a bit of butter in the cupboard and had a nice supper. When Mrs Pagles came home on the Friday I gave her sixpence to put in the 'babby's' money box. She thanked me very much and made me a cup of cocoa.

11

Carriages without horses shall run,
And to an end the world will come,
In eighteen hundred and eighty-one.
(Mother Shipton)

Each day after Christmas the weather got worse and worse with bitter north winds, so I was always glad to get home and sit by Mrs Pagles's fire and listen to her talk. She would let me talk now and then and I'd tell her about things that happened in the shops where I had worked. I wanted to tell her about little Fanny 'Topknot' at the college, but I was afraid she would laugh at me.

Once she started talking she never seemed to want to leave off or go to bed. I didn't mind, it was nice and warm sitting there. Sometimes I dozed off for a bit and when I woke up she was still going. She liked best to tell me about when she was a little girl and lived in the country.

Her father did iron work for farmers and her mother was always having babies, and as Mrs Pagles was the eldest she had to carry the babies about. When the school holidays came, she had to cart a baby about all the time. She would go across the fields and when she was out of sight of her cottage, she would dump the baby down under a hedge and play with the other girls, climbing trees and sliding down the branches to the ground, crawling through culverts under roads, always afraid they might get stuck there and never get out.

Best of all was to find a deep dry ditch and roof it over with boughs of trees and ferns, and so make a little house where they sat and told tales. The other girls used to laugh at her because her stockings were always coming down; she used bits of rag for garters but didn't tie the knots properly. Her clothes got in an awful mess but it didn't matter because they were only old things she wore in the holidays. On Sunday her mother dressed her up ever so smart in a nice velvet dress, and as she walked through the village to church she used to look out of the corner of her eye to see if anyone was noticing her from the cottage windows. They seldom had fresh meat for dinner and never had milk to drink — it was like begging to get a farmer to sell you some. Some days for dinner they had bacon pudding and ate it standing up. The children never sat down to dinner but just golloped up anything that was going and ran out to play. Her mother made nice bacon pudding. She rolled out some dough and laid pieces of fat streaky bacon on it and then rolled it up like a roly-poly and wrapped it in a cloth and boiled it. When it got cold, a thick slice did for dinner. Many times since she left home she had 'longed her heart out' for a piece of that pudding, and once before her baby came her mother sent her a lump by post. Then she'd tell me about when she came to London to be a servant and met Mr Pagles who 'was *such* a gentleman'.

She said that one of her sisters who was sixteen might come up to London soon and stay with her until she got a situation. She said that her sister was very pretty and it wouldn't be long before she got a nice young man. I said that I should be glad if she did come, because I'd begun to think that girls were nicer to talk to than boys. I might go for walks with her on Sunday and get friendly — perhaps she wouldn't talk so much as her sister did — lots of boys used to walk with girls up Rye Lane on Sunday nights, and some of the girls didn't look more than fourteen.

Now I will tell you about the most unpleasant job I ever had. One day early in January, Mr Gaynibb ordered me to go to the police court in South London to help prosecute two little boys who had stolen something from his shop. It was while I had gone to dinner, and as there was very little trade about after Christmas instead of being behind the counter he had sat in the back parlour. Two boys crept in and took a shilling bullseye lantern off the counter. As they went out a detective who had been watching their movements stopped them and brought them back. The detective asked Mr Gaynibb to prosecute them and he consented. All he had to do was to send someone to the police court to identify the lantern, so I had to go next morning. I was used to police courts because I'd gone in one in Swansea many times and listened to cases, but I never thought I should ever be in a case myself. The little boys were about twelve years old and were quite decently dressed, but they did look so pale and frightened, staring at the detective while he was telling the magistrate what they'd done.

Then I had to go in the witness box and swear to tell the truth and then answer questions. I told the court that my name was Thomas Lloyd, that I was employed by the prosecutor.

'Take this lantern in your hand. Do you identify that as the property of your employer?' I said, 'Yes, sir,' to all the questions and kept looking at the boys kindly — I wanted them to know that it wasn't me that wanted them punished. I was only doing what I was made to do. Then the policeman standing by the witness box told me to turn and face the magistrate when I was speaking, and the magistrate looked at me as if he would like to lock me up too.

Then we all waited while the magistrate made up his mind. When he had, he told the boys that they would be remanded to the workhouse for a week and then brought up again. The fathers of the boys came forward, respectable-looking men dressed in shabby best clothes and looking pale and nervous. They begged the magistrate to let their sons out on bail and not send them to the workhouse. 'I've got a good home to take my boy to, your Worship.' But he wouldn't, so the boys were taken away crying and their mothers cried as well. I felt like it too because I thought of things that I had done when I was those boys' age that I hadn't been copped for.

As I went back to the shop I thought that perhaps a week in the workhouse would punish them so much that they'd never steal anything ever again, but if I'd been the magistrate I'd have given them a 'hander' or two like I'd had in school — they wouldn't forget that.

I didn't have to go to the court next week, but the detective came and told Mr Gaynibb that those poor little chaps had been sent to a reformatory for four years. Four years for a toy lantern! I wonder what they'd have got if they'd nicked a railway sleeper?

Soon after that came the greatest snow-storm I ever saw. It was on a Tuesday in the middle of January and because of the loss of life and suffering it caused it was called 'Black Tuesday' afterwards.

The storm was general all over England, and many poor people were buried in snow drifts and some died. It started snowing before I opened the shop and then came a regular blizzard. Clouds of snow blew into the shop faster than I could sweep it out. It was fine powdery snow like flour, and the wind drove it into every crack or crevice, under slats and tiles, under street doors and through key holes and letter-boxes. It made piles of snow on the door mats inside houses and it didn't melt as snow does when it gets indoors. That'll show you how cold it was. Masses of it stayed unmelted for a week or more under the roof slates and when it did melt ceilings fell down. The wind drifted it so strongly that while one side of a road would be quite clear, the shops on the other side were in a drift over six feet high. The few people who were about could hardly move against the wind and they were soon covered from head to foot by the snow.

It was no good shutting our shop door, the snow came under it, so Mr Gaynibb told me to put the shutters up again and he'd close the 'something' shop for the day. I got covered with snow doing that, but it didn't matter as it brushed off like dust.

After that I had to go and buy things for their dinner and then to the public house for some beer (with two little bottles in my pocket for rum) and Mrs Gaynibb called me on one side privately and gave me a bottle to get her half a pint of gin. I was surprised because I thought she was a teetotaller as the Guv'nor was so afraid of her seeing him have a little drop on the quiet.

Then they told me I could have the day off. By this time the snow was piled against the shop fronts in Rye Lane as high as the names over the windows, and you couldn't see which was pavement or which was road. I got over to the other side and by hugging close to the shops with my head down I managed to fight against the wind. As I got near the corner I was blown to a standstill and had to cling to the railings of a church there.

A poor little fox terrier was blown round towards me. The wind was blowing its hind part right round in front of its head. It looked back to see who had kicked it, but seeing nobody it lost its temper and bit savagely at the wind.

It looked so sad at me when I burst out laughing but I couldn't help it. Once round the corner it was easier going and Sumner Road wasn't far. When I got home I found the cottage was snowed up too, and Mrs Pagles came to a bedroom window when I shouted. I asked her to throw out a coal shovel and a broom so that I could clear the snow away and dig a way in. She was glad I came home because she hadn't been able to go out and buy anything. So I went and got her some milk for the baby, and potatoes. She was as grateful as the travellers on the Alps are to St Bernard dogs. She said she hadn't the heart to wake her husband, he had come home dead tired. She *was* a good little wife. If I'd been old enough I should have liked to be married to her if she didn't talk so much, but I didn't suppose that affected her husband, him being asleep all day.

If I'd been married to her I wouldn't have got a night job like he had. It seemed a funny way to go on, and I wouldn't have cared about it, especially in the cold weather. But it was no use me thinking about things like that. I'd been told that a man mustn't get married until he's twenty-one, and I was only sixteen, but I couldn't help wondering about things.

After I had had a good warm by her fire, she gave me some pea soup, nice and hot, and after that she wanted to make me a cup of cocoa but I didn't fancy it — not on top of the soup.

I started wondering what I'd better do. It seemed a pity to waste such an unexpected holiday. It was too cold to go in my bedroom and if I sat reading by her fire she'd keep talking all the time. So I thought I would try to get up to a theatre in south London and see a pantomime. The wind wasn't so bad in the afternoon but it was still snowing and there weren't any trams or buses running. Many people had cleaned the snow from the pavements and gangs of men earned a bit by piling the snow into parapets five feet high alongside the roads.

It took me over an hour to get to the theatre and then I was too early, so I went in a coffee shop and had some tea and stayed there till six o'clock. There were only a few people waiting at the gallery entrance so I made sure that I'd get a good seat right in the front row.

There wasn't any crush going in, but we had to wait nearly an hour before the show commenced. Then a gentleman came before the curtains and made a speech. He asked the audience to excuse the delay, but the principal actors couldn't get there because of the traffic breakdown, but some of the others were there and 'with ladies' and gentlemen's kind permission they would endeavour to do the best they could.' So the people shouted, 'Hear, hear. Bravo and carry on.'

When they did start you could see there was going to be some fun. The actors who took the best parts didn't know the words but read them from sheets of paper. Some of them read their bits to each other at the same time, and you could hear someone shouting directions to them from the side of the stage. Two girls walked on before their time and a man behind the curtain shouted, 'Come orf!'

When they sang the songs they got on better; they were popular music hall songs that everyone knew. There were only about ten of us in the gallery and about twenty in the pit. I couldn't see if anyone was in the dress circle. I never saw a big theatre so empty. We clapped and stamped at everything they did on the stage — but it was as much to get warm as anything — it was jolly cold up there.

There was another long wait when the curtain went down on the first scene. They changed the scenery, but when they started again things got more mixed up than ever. We couldn't tell what the show was about. They gave up trying to keep to the book and made up things to say as they went along, and while we were laughing at them they were laughing at each other — talk about pantomime! It was funnier than any I had ever seen.

At the end of the scene the gentleman came out again and said it was impossible to continue owing to the absence of so many of the company, but with our kind permission they would entertain us with a few single turns. In the meantime, he would send some hot coffee to the patrons in the gallery and pit. We cheered and clapped at that and soon an attendant came with a large jug of coffee and some cups — and that coffee went down a treat.

The first turn was announced as Miss Cora de Vere. She was a tall girl with nice legs and had tights on. She said that 'with our kind permission she would give us a song, which owing to today's weather we might think appropriate.' It was about some girl named Nellie who had got herself lost on a snowy day and her chap went out and found her. I only remember the chorus:

> I traced her little footmarks in the snow
> (don't yer know?)
> Traced her little footmarks in the snow.

> I shan't forget the day
> When Nellie lost her way,
> And I traced her little footmarks in the snow.

We all laughed and gave that girl a good clap, but I know that if it had snowed like it did today when Nellie got lost there wouldn't have been any footmarks in the snow, it'd have gone right up the poor girl's legs.

There were a few more songs and dances and then the show ended at ten o'clock. On the way home I bought some baked chestnuts and as I ate them going along I thought about the exciting day I had had and reckoned that I never would forget Black Tuesday.

Soon after the great snowstorm, Mr Gaynibb must have found his money hard to hold again. He bought a row of cottages in a back street in Peckham and was going to retire from business once more. All he'd have to do was to go and collect rents every Monday morning. He said, 'There's nothing like bricks and mortar. Safe as houses as the saying is — I've had a good offer and as the missis wants to live private again I've taken it — but you'll be all right, Tom. I've spoken to the new people about you and they'll keep you on if you like to stop.'

I was sorry to hear that he was going. I liked him so much and he'd always treated me more like a chum than his shop boy. I was sorry too to think that he was going to be a landlord; being a landlord wasn't all 'raspberry'. If he knew some of the things landlords had to put up with he'd have thought twice about it. They were a rather rough lot down that neighbourhood, and what with the way some tenants went on and his temper and language, there were likely to be some lively scenes in that street. He had sworn at me many times but I'd never taken any notice any more than if it had been the parrot. I'd heard it said that if the employer is a little blind and the servant a little deaf, things go on pretty smoothly.

I didn't know it at the time, but I heard afterwards that he had made it a condition that I was to be kept on if I wanted to. So that shows you what a nice old chap he was.

Mr Carwynne, my new employer, had a small wholesale toy business in the city and a stall at the Crystal Palace. He went up to his office most days and his wife and I looked after the shop. His old aunt did the housework. Mrs Carwynne was a tall fair lady about thirty. She had beautiful large eyes and a lot of fluffy hair, rather auburn. I liked her directly I saw her and learned a lot by noticing how she dealt with customers.

Mr Gaynibb had sold off all the shabby stock, and the new stock that Mr Carwynne brought in was much better class. He dressed the windows better and trade soon improved. I liked to watch Mrs Carwynne serving customers, especially if they were men — her eyes helped her a lot then because they never went away without buying.

It didn't matter how troublesome customers were, she never lost patience and seldom lost a sale, and lots of times she got them to buy a more expensive article than they came in for. She had such a way of pointing out the quality and beauty of an article, looking at them all the time with her nice eyes, that the customer couldn't help agreeing with her. After she'd said how uncommon or artistic the thing was, she'd say, 'You *do* think so — don't you, Madam?' as if she was only echoing their opinion about the article she was showing them.

I think she must have mesmerised them or something and made the customers go away feeling that the thing they had just bought was something they had been looking for for years. When she got their money, she always said, 'Thank you *so* much,' just as if she meant it. She was never idle. She filled up spare time by knitting. In twenty minutes she would knit a wool 'Princess robe' and a little bonnet for a sixpenny waxfaced doll, and then put it in the window and sell it for half a crown. She did lots of those and they were never in the window long.

Trade got better and better and I had plenty to do. Afternoons and evenings were the busiest times. I noticed some evenings that she would ask customers to allow her to send the things they bought, on the next morning; and I saw afterwards that it wasn't done to oblige them so much. It was so that I could take her little son out for a morning walk when I took the parcel.

So she was artful as well as beautiful. Her son, Charley, was a dear little chap under three years old. I was rather proud to hold his hand and walk with him. He had a white starched dress with nice embroidery on it, a white petticoat and white things underneath. I was asked to unbutton the underneath things in case of emergency but I never once was quick enough, not being used to it, so I didn't save her much in laundry bills!

Mr Carwynne made much more profit on toys than Mr Gaynibb did. He imported most of them from Nuremburg and sometimes went to Germany buying. He told me once that whole families including the children made those toys in their own little houses, getting the wood for nothing in the Black Forest. Then the toys were collected and sent to dealers in Nuremburg who exported them to England. He said that the German children got as much fun out of making the things as our children did in playing with them.

Just before Easter, Mrs Carwynne asked me if I would care to go with them to the Crystal Palace on bank holiday to help at their stall for a time, and then have the evening off to see the sights. They could get me in free and would pay my railway fare.

I had to go to the shop early on Easter Monday and collect two large parcels of toys and then catch a train about nine o'clock. The parcels were light but very bulky and there wasn't room in any carriage so I had to go in the guard's van. Many times after that I had to travel in the guard's van, the carriages being so crowded. The Palace was so popular on holidays; it suited most people because wet or fine there was plenty of room for thousands and always some entertainment going on. There was no place like it near London, and sixty thousand visitors on a bank holiday was nothing out of the way.

Our stall was on the ground floor in a bay between two large stairways that came from the main floor of the Palace down towards the grounds, so there was a constant stream of visitors passing to and fro. The stall had three sides; Mrs Carwynne managed the centre and most important part, while Mr Carwynne and I looked after a side each.

We were not very busy in the morning, but later when people came flocking in from the gardens we sold lots of toys and things for presents. Once the people got in they didn't want to go down all those stone steps to the grounds again, so they wandered about inside looking at the sights and buying things.

When dinner time came, they told me to go to the second-class dining rooms where by showing my staff ticket I could get served at a reduced price. So I had some cold beef, pickles and bread for ninepence.

As no gaslights were allowed downstairs in case of fire, we had to close the stall when it got too dark to see plainly. The Palace people were much afraid of fire. Nobody was allowed to smoke on the ground floors, and there were notices all about saying, 'No Smoking Allowed' and 'Défence de Fumer'.

When we shut up shop I went upstairs to see things. Only the centre part was illuminated. The side courts where the statues were seemed quite dark, but they were the most crowded. Lots of young men and girls passed up and down all the time and jostled each other. Many couples were sitting in dark corners, and passers-by made remarks to tease them. 'I'll tell your Mother, Maudie,' and 'Anything like that you *can* enjoy,' but nobody took offence. Everybody was enjoying themselves and all was jolly.

It was too dark to see the statuary properly, so next time I went to the Palace I took something to eat with me and spent my dinner time looking at them. They were true copies of some of the most beautiful sculpture in the world and quite worth the shilling admission to see them alone. I liked those of ladies best and could hardly believe that ladies could look so beautiful when they had nothing on, so smooth and soft looking, not all knobbly like boys are.

I went again on Whit Monday and on other days when fetes were held there. There was the Foresters' Fete, the Odd-Fellows and the Hearts of Oak, and also a great gathering of Temperance people. Tens of thousands came and we sold heaps of things. I liked the Sunday school treats best, such a lot of boys and girls all dressed in their best. Most of the girls had white dresses with pretty sashes — their mothers must have had a time, getting them up like that. Nearly all had money to spend, and as Mrs Carwynne had taught me to hammer out 'Pop Goes the Weasel' and a bit of 'The Last Rose of Summer' on a sixpenny dulcimer, I soon had a lot of those kids round and sold them a dulcimer or some other toy.

The Palace people would not allow the stall keepers to shout out to draw attention to their goods. You had to wait until someone enquired the price or stopped to examine things. But Mrs Carwynne got over that in her artful way. I was to wait until a few gathered round and then pick up a doll or something and look at it as if astonished and then say loudly, 'Are you sure, Ma'am, that this is only sixpence?' and she would reply, 'Yes, Tom. We'll let it go for that today.' We sold many more things that way. She was a clever wife for a business man to have. I often wished she wasn't married.

One bank holiday I found a large parcel of false whiskers under the stall. They had been put away as unsaleable a long time ago, but they were quite good imitations. Each had a big moustache and two long side-whiskers with hooks to go over your ears. I think they called them 'Dundrearys' or 'Piccadilly Weepers'. I thought I'd try to sell some and Mrs Carwynne persuaded me to put on a pair to draw attention. She took a lot of trouble to pick a pair that suited my colour and fixed it nicely for me. As my hair was rather curly, the hooks didn't show.

I must have looked about thirty when I had those on and girls and people kept looking wonderingly at me and nudging each other to look. I didn't care, but kept them on all the afternoon, and by calling out to Mrs Carwynne now and then to ask if these splendid pairs of whiskers were only a shilling each I sold the lot to young men and big boys before tea time. The upshot was that later on you couldn't go anywhere about the Palace without coming across those whiskers. Some of the fellows had them on upside-down with the side bits sticking up each side of their head. They had plenty of fun with them that night in the side courts. Some cheeky girls would snatch them off, and either wear them themselves or run away with them screaming, with the chap after them.

Our stall certainly helped to make things jolly that day and I wished I had bought my pair instead of selling them — then I might have had a girl to chase.

One day when I was having dinner at Colepeter's I saw in a newspaper that the Jewish schools in the East End were going to have a treat at the Crystal Palace. I made a note of the date and asked Mr Carwynne if he knew about it. I was glad I told him because the Jews hadn't been there before and he hadn't got it down in his book like the other fetes.

Mrs Carwynne and I went there on that date and, my word, we did have a time with those Jewish kids. They weren't dressed up so well as the Sunday school groups, but they did come from the slums. Some of the girls had velvet dresses and some silk, but most of the others were a bit shabby, especially the boys. But they all had money to spend and instead of going round looking at the sights lots of them swarmed round the stalls where things were being sold. If they weren't buying anything themselves they would crowd round when some other kid was choosing something. They would either tell him not to buy it, or pick up some other thing and tell him that it was better value. Sometimes half a dozen would pick up things at the same time and say, 'How much this, Guv'nor?' So I had to watch out.

On that day we had a lot of new things to do conjuring tricks with. One was a little tin cylinder. You covered a dice with it and then when you lifted the cylinder up again there was a pile of six ha'pennies there. (There was only one ha'penny really. It was stuck on top of five copper rings that looked like the rims of coins.) When you went to put the dice under it, you lifted the cylinder out and pinched it and so lifted the concealed 'coins' as well. They were a shilling each and I had to do the trick before a crowd of Jewish boys many times before I sold one.

One boy offered me ninepence, but I told him that it was only elevenpence-ha'penny he'd be paying really, because of the ha'penny stuck on the coins. I think that helped to make the first sale, because that ha'penny could be knocked off and spent after the toy was worn out. I told him too that the proper price was 1s 6d and this was the only one left. I did have a job, but he bought it at last. I soon found that I had made a mistake by saying it was the only one we'd got left, because a lot of the other boys went after him and they got him up in a corner by the ivory stall and tried to buy it off him at a small profit. The young lady at the ivory stall said she never heard such a row as they made, and at last the boy got them to bid against each other and sold the thing for 1s 2½d.

I didn't show any more of those tricks until that little crowd had cleared off, but I soon learned their game. I sold a few later on by asking 1s 3d and saying that they were reduced from 1s 6d each, and then I took their money if they offered a shilling. After a lot of talk to each other, two little boys clubbed together and paid sixpence each to get one between them, but they came back soon after and one of them wanted me to give him his sixpence back because the other boy wouldn't let him mind the thing. The other boy said, 'You can have it when I done with it, what more you want?' Other boys gathered round and took sides and as it was stopping business I took the conjuring trick back and gave one boy a 6*d* dulcimer and the other a clockwork mouse. I don't think King Solomon could have done anything different. I soon found that I'd made another mistake. It got to be known that I was changing things and many of them who had got all the fun they wanted out of some toy they had bought brought it back and wanted to change it for something else. When I refused, they'd offer to sell it back to me for 5*d* or 4½*d* and couldn't understand why I wouldn't buy it. 'You can sell it again for sixpence,' they'd say. One boy who'd got tired of his sixpenny dulcimer hung about the stall until he saw me about to sell one, and then he pushed in and sold his to the other boy for fivepence. Three boys did this and I lost some sales. Then they got wise to me putting the price up and then reducing it, and when I asked eightpence for a sixpenny article they'd say, 'Garn, yer trying to jew us.'

I had a worrying time that morning, and all the time two little girls from their school treat stood by the stall and looked on. They were both about thirteen and rather chubby but pretty, with large dark eyes, long eyelashes and a lot of brown hair, something like Rebecca in *Ivanhoe* must have looked when she was a little girl. I couldn't help liking them. They came to the stall quite early and asked the price of nearly everything on it. I showed them how things worked, played the dulcimer and made dolls shut their eyes, but they never bought anything. I began to think that they hadn't any money and were doing it for a lark, but they looked too serious and innocent for that, so I gave it up. But they still stayed at the end of the stall looking on. I felt sorry that the little things should waste their holiday, and asked them why they didn't go out and see the pretty fountains playing and other sights in the Palace. They said, 'We like to see you selling things.' It seemed funny that little children should stop to look at business being done instead of going about and enjoying themselves. The girls over at the scent stall noticed them and pointed them out to the young lady at the ivory stall, and they kept giggling at me and pointing to those two kids. Then Mrs Carwynne started on me. She said, 'I *am* surprised, Tom. Two at a time!' and later on, 'You'll have to see them home, Tom. They'll never leave you.'

I felt angry with everybody for a time, but I couldn't be sulky with Mrs Carwynne for long — she was only joking.

They were such nice little things that I hadn't the heart to be rude and tell them to bunk off, so when I wasn't serving I told them that they ought to go in the Gallery and see the Wurtemburg Collection of Stuffed Animals. They were so funny; little kittens, frogs, rabbits, moles and squirrels, and similar things, all dressed up like ordinary children and people. They were put in models of houses and inns and made to look as if they were doing things like human beings. But I only wasted my time. They just stared at me all the time I was telling them. I thought then that perhaps they weren't 'all there'. Anyhow, they still hung about until a teacher came collecting girls to go and have tea. When Mrs Carwynne counted up the takings she said we'd had a very good day and she hoped the Jewish schools would come every year. I hoped so too. They were a bit of a worry, but they had money to spend and seemed to enjoy spending it. They weren't as well dressed as the Sunday school children, but they looked better fed, and many were much better looking, especially the girls.

That was the last of the 'Treat' season so the big stall was closed and only a small one kept open with a girl in charge.

12

It was when the cistern at our shop went wrong that I got to know Bob Shipside. He worked for a plumber up Rye Lane, and went with him when he had repairs to do in houses, handing him the tools and helping as much as he could. We got friendly and after that went about together. He was the only boy I knew as a friend in Peckham. Although he was a year younger he was taller than me, but perhaps he was the proper size and I was shorter than most boys my age. Anyhow, we got on well together.

I used to tell him about the Palace and other jobs I'd had, but he wasn't very good at listening though he wanted me to listen to him when he talked about drains and the different houses he went to, and the servant girls he'd got to know when he went to mend the pipes. He said he could have a different girl to walk out with every Sunday if he liked. I thought he could too – he was very good-looking, although I thought my curly hair was my best point. He said he hadn't seen any girl he'd like to stick to. The nicest ones went up and down Rye Lane on Sunday night, he said, and they always went in pairs. You couldn't very well get talking unless you had another boy with you. So I said I'd come with him next Sunday.

Before I knew Bob I often saw some girl up Rye Lane who I would have liked to talk to, but she always had another girl with her and I had nobody to introduce me; but when I went with Bob it was quite easy. He'd just accidentally push against them in passing and then apologise. They'd say, 'Granted, I'm sure,' and after that it was 'all Sir Garnet'. The only thing was that he always managed to pal on to the best looking one while I had to take what was left. I never saw two nice-looking ones together. I suppose the pretty one took the other girl with her so as to show herself off more, while the plain one used the other girl as a 'call bird'.

In the summer you could make a selection beforehand, but on dark winter evenings you had to wait until you got to the next street lamp before you could get a good look — and I didn't have much luck. According to the 'rules' you walked with them to the top of Rye Lane and back, and if it was rather late you saw them home. They never troubled you to come farther than the top of their street. It was generally quite a swell road with trees, but they didn't really live there at all, but in another street that they didn't think much of. If the girls didn't fancy your company much, they never said so. They suddenly remembered that they had to be home by nine and would stop and shake hands at the corner of the next street. Then if half an hour later you saw them walking on the other side of Rye Lane you pretended not to see them. It was quite understood — all very 'genteel' and polite.

The girls weren't very truthful either. They didn't stop at deceiving you about where they lived — a girl's name would be Clare de Laney, her father an engineer, and her job would be to give music lessons. Later on you heard that she was Ada Lane and she worked at Pink's Jam Factory.

It was a bit of a job to know what to talk about as you went along with them. They didn't help much — only giggle. But if you bought some 'Conversation Lozenges' that helped a lot. They were round flat peppermints with words printed on them in red, 'When's your birthday?' and 'You are sweet', or 'Are you engaged?' and a lot of other silly stuff. So I got to know several girls after I met Bob. But it was a bit awkward when some of them came up Rye Lane on week nights and saw me at the shop door, because I always told them that I was a clerk in the office of the Crystal Palace.

133

My friendship with Bob Shipside came to an end soon after he got a job as railway porter at Whitechapel station. He was only getting twelve shillings a week as plumber's mate, so just for the sake of getting a little more money he gave up the chance to learn a good trade. He told me that he was going to have sixteen shillings a week, a suit of working clothes and a safe job for life. He asked me to take the train from Peckham Rye and come to see him some Sunday afternoon. He looked after the station all by himself on Sunday, and as he took the tickets from the passengers he said I'd be all right. So I took a penny ticket to the next station, and went to see him.

His work was very interesting and at first I envied him. There weren't many trains running on Sunday, but I helped him to shut carriage doors and yell out 'Whitechapel!' Then we sat in the Porters' Room and talked. But I got away rather early because the smoke from the trains and the fumes from the tunnel made it very smelly and sulphury down in that station. So I went out and had a walk up Whitechapel Road. The pavements there were full of foreign-looking people promenading up and down. Rye Lane 'wasn't in it' for dress. Lots of pretty Jewesses with fine heads of hair, and all of them dressed in the latest. I went a good way along and looked out for those little Jew girls I saw in the Palace. Each time I went to Whitechapel I did that, but I never found them, and soon after I left off going to see Bob. He'd got a bit nasty because I went out instead of staying down in that smelly station with him all the time.

Having no one to go about with on Sundays and wondering what to do with myself all day, I suddenly remembered that I had promised the jeweller's lady that I would go to their church. I kept my word but I only went once and sat right at the back near the door. It was a new church and smelt of varnish, and it had the same sort of service as those churches in north London had where I used to go on wet Sunday mornings. I didn't care about it much — getting up and repeating things — I expect it's all right if you'd got used to it when you were young, but I hadn't. When the sermon came I didn't pay much attention. I got thinking back to that old church in Berkshire where I saw Fanny 'Topknot' Tingey — and the pigs. I thought about those boys at the college and how educated I should have been if I could have stopped there — but what poor food we had, and not enough of it. Of course, I saw now why the other boys didn't look half starved — they had plenty of pocket money and bought things to eat outside, while I only had a sixpence and spent that first go. The things that had happened to me since I left that school! It was only seven years ago, and what was going to happen in the next seven years? I ought to have stuck to the boot trade — what a fool! What's the good of going on week after week working in a toy shop for seventeen shillings a week — a girl's job! Mrs Carwynne said they'd never employed a boy before, only girls or young women. I'd better look out for something else with more prospects. Perhaps it would be better to get into the grocery trade — there were only men in that and the grocery business wouldn't be likely to 'get the knock'. People would always want tea and sugar and things grocers sold. Yes, and I knew a bit about that trade when I was a kid in our shop. I might get taken on as a learner if I went for little money, and grocers' assistants always 'lived in'. So I'd get food and lodging. But, if I gave notice, I might never see Mrs Carwynne any more! She was always so kind to me, and little Charley too. I should miss him. When I teased him in fun, he'd get red and angry and hit at me with his little fists and say, 'You debble, Tom,' but he always came and kissed me good night.

Perhaps when I'd gone far away and years had gone by, they'd sit by the fire and talk sadly of that poor boy Tom who used to take little Charley for walks and tell him little tales. I felt very sorry for myself.

Then the sermon was over and I went outside feeling sad and sniffy. I didn't go to that church again. I hadn't promised to keep on going. So next Sunday I walked a long way up the

Old Kent Road and went to a Wesleyan church where quite a young man preached a nice sermon.

I had read somewhere about John Wesley and how he'd disagreed with the regular church and started one of his own. So I went to see what the difference was. I had begun to feel rather religious about that time and thought I would try to find out for myself which was the right one. There seemed so many different sects, each of them believing they were the only right one.

I peeped in to the downstairs part of that church, but it was full of very well dressed people. So I went upstairs to a gallery where there were only a few. I had a very long seat all to myself and in the seat on the other side of the gangway was a lady who looked about nineteen. After a little while she came across and gave me a hymn book. I didn't want one really, not being much of a singer, but I thanked her just the same. I read the words of the thing they were singing; it was the 'Te Deum', and a little later they sang 'Jubilate Deo' and I liked that best – it was more rollicky. While they were singing, I looked across at that young lady. She wasn't what you'd call pretty, but she had a lot of dark hair that looked nice, and she wasn't so well dressed as the people downstairs, but what she had on was neat and looked good. But if she wasn't pretty she had a good voice to make up for it. It was a contralto and rang out clear and beautiful above all the others. I hadn't heard such a voice since I left Wales.

When the minister started talking, he spoke out better than the church one did. It wasn't a very long sermon but it was one you could remember. It was about the power of example, and 'avoiding things whereby your brother stumbleth'. After he had explained it a bit, I saw that it didn't mean that if you saw your brother fall over a brick you should avoid doing the same. You might laugh at them, but you wouldn't be so silly as that. As the preacher put it, it didn't mean your brother only, but any fellow. They were all your brothers. He never said anything about all girls being your sisters. I thought it was just as well they weren't.

Anyhow, I'd never had any brothers and didn't want any, not if they might be like some of the fellows I'd met with.

Well, if this man who was your brother was going to do something that wouldn't be good for him to do, and you were going to do it as well, and if you thought that if he did it he mightn't do it as well as you did it, it would be better if you didn't do it at all, and then if you didn't, he wouldn't. (I wish I were educated enough to explain it to you better.) When he came to the finish, it appeared that the thing to avoid was Drink. You yourself might be able to drink Drink and leave off drinking it when you'd had enough, but the other chap might go on drinking Drink until he got tipsy. So it was better for you to avoid drinking Drink altogether and then the other man might follow your example and chuck it too.

Perhaps this isn't quite the way he put it, but that's how I understood it. It was quite a good sermon but it didn't affect me because I hadn't drunk any Drink for a long time – not since Mr Gaynibb went, and then it was only the drain of rum left in his little bottle.

Next Sunday morning I went there again, and that girl was there, just the same, all alone in her seat. I didn't pick up any hymn book, so when they gave out the hymns she came across and handed me a book all opened ready at the proper page. I whispered softly, 'Thank you *so* much,' and took a good look at her. She had nice brown eyes that looked full of kindness – the sort of look that my landlady had sometimes when she was looking at her baby and talking silly to it. I never saw her look like that to her husband or me – it must be a special look that women keep for things they like best of all.

But I thought that girl must always have had that sort of look; being religious and good, she felt kind to everybody. She caught me looking at her several times, and I am afraid I didn't pay much attention to the service. I kept wondering about her. (Why didn't she have anyone with her? A young man, or a little brother or sister. Perhaps she's a lonely one like me. I wonder what she'd say if I waited outside and took off my hat to her. If I could only get to talk to her for a minute. How would it be if I went in her pew next Sunday and sat side of her? I wonder what she'd think — she couldn't make any fuss about it, not in church. I might put a conversation lozenge on the ledge in front, just near where she could see it, that one with 'Are You Engaged?' on it. No, better not. She might be shocked at such a thing in church. Sacrilege or something. Another thing, if I sat side of her she'd find out I couldn't sing and I shouldn't like to stand alongside a nice girl when they were singing the 'Te Deum' — there's a bit in that that I didn't think quite nice.

No, better leave it till I get outside. It would be *all right* if I could get chummy with her. Then I'd show 'em something up Rye Lane, a fine tall young woman like her. Better than those bits of kids with their little bustles on behind, wagging up and down.)

Then the minister left off and I got up quickly, but just as I was hurrying down the stairs two old gentlemen stopped me on the landing. They said, 'Good morning' and 'How do you do' and shook hands with me. Then they asked me some questions. What was my name and if I belonged to the Wesleyan Society, and would I join. They were pleased to welcome me and so on. I was so bewildered that I gave them my real name and address, but I wouldn't promise anything. I wasn't going to get bound down. I'd find out more about religion before I joined anything. They were kind-looking men, but they frightened me away, so I never went again. When I got outside, that girl had gone, so I never saw her again either, but I often thought of her.

On two Sundays after that I went to the Roman Catholic church in Peckham Park Road because I heard a man on Peckham Rye preaching about it. He said it was the only true Church and Saint Peter was the first Pope and Bishop of Rome. I didn't understand anything I heard there, and the smoky smell wasn't nice. After that I went to Kennington and heard the Rev. Mr Baxter — he was even stronger than the Christadelphians in telling us of the awful things that were going to happen in a year or two before the world came to an end, which would be quite soon. I did hear that he had just renewed the lease of his house, but perhaps that was only a tale. Anyhow he seemed sincere, and the hall was crowded.

Then I left off going anywhere, but bought a Bible off a stall and thought I'd find out about religion by reading that carefully. It had very good print and fine engravings in it, so it wasn't dear for threepence.

I meant to read right through from the beginning, but I soon found that I had to skip many dry pages and pick out chapters here and there that told of wonderful and magical things, like there are in the *Arabian Nights* and just as hard to believe in. The Jews seemed to have a God of their own to help them in the wars they were always having with their neighbours — when they won a battle they praised God for it. When they got licked it wasn't because the enemy were too many for them, it was 'God punishing them for their sins'.

There was one fine picture in that book showing the inside of a tent where a woman named Jael was killing a man called Sisera. He was a Captain of something, and had been beaten in a battle, so he came all tired out to Jael's tent to rest, 'because he was at peace with her people'. So Jael let him lay on her couch and gave him a bottle of milk to drink. And then when he'd gone to sleep, she got a hammer and drove a nail right through his head. She was thought a lot of for doing that. I couldn't understand why, and I didn't fancy the Jewish girls so much after reading that.

I found the Book of Esther the most interesting, and I wondered why Shakespeare didn't make a play out of it. There's nothing about God or religion in it and it looks as if it was written just to show off how a Jewess got to be a Queen in Persia or somewhere.

Some parts of it are quite funny, especially that bit where King Ahasuerus sent out letters to all the cities and provinces to say 'that every man shall be master in his own house'.

139

You see, the king was giving a dinner to a lot of other kings from round about and he sent for Queen Vashti to come and show herself off to them. But the queen refused to come, so those kings got frightened about what would happen when their wives heard of what Queen Vashti had done. They might get to be disobedient like her and it would 'lead to contempt' and rows. So King Ahasuerus sent notices to all the far places so that 'the wives and the ladies of Persia should understand that every man shall be master in his own house'.

Then Queen Vashti got the sack and it was given out that there was a vacancy for a new queen. So an old Jew named Mordecai got his niece Esther to apply for the job. On no account was she to let on that she was a Jewess, because somehow Jews weren't liked much in that country. Before she applied she had to be washed, and it says, 'When she was washed she was very fair and beautiful,' but it took weeks before she was nice enough.

So Esther got to be queen and her Uncle Mordecai spent his time hanging round the palace gates. Once Esther sent him some new clothes but they got pinched on the way.

Then a man named Haman, who was a big pot about the Palace got annoyed because Mordecai wouldn't salute him when he went in or out. So Haman got King Ahasuerus to order that all the Jews were to be murdered. Before this was done, Esther heard about it, so she wheedled round the king to cancel the order and Haman got killed instead. But I expect you have read the Book of Esther and wondered at it being written so seriously considering how funny some of it was.

I didn't find anything to make me feel religious in the Old part, but when I got to the New Testament I had to read it through more than once, and thought that if everyone followed its simple teaching things would be better in the world. But I couldn't believe in the miracle of the Gadarene Swine, and I thought that nightmare at the end might just as well have been left out.

13

When the Crystal Palace season was over, Mrs Carwynne left off coming into the shop to serve customers. Mr Carwynne had to stop going to the City and he took her place behind the counter. He was almost as nice to me as Mrs Carwynne was, but he didn't talk to me as much as she did unless business was rather slack on wet days. Then he would tell me many things about Germany and the toy trade. He said he liked selling toys better than any other business. It wasn't like some trades where things were sold that might do harm if taken in excess. (I expect he meant drink or tobacco.) He said that everything you sold in a toy shop gave pleasure all round. The people who bought the toys felt happy and kind, and the thing they bought couldn't help giving pleasure to some little child. It was an innocent trade and nothing they sold would do harm. It was a nice thought of his and showed his kindly nature. I had never thought of it in that way, but afterwards I remembered a sad piece of poetry I had read somewhere. It was by Max Adder and about a little boy named Willie. I didn't tell it to Mr Carwynne; I was afraid he might get worrying about little Charley. But I'm sure Mr Adder won't mind me repeating it to you.

Willie had a purple monkey climbing on a yellow
    stick,
And when he licked the paint all off it made him
    deathly sick,

In his latest hour he clasped that monkey in his
   hand,
And bade good-bye to earth and went into a better
   land.

Oh! No more he'll shoot his sister with his little
   wooden gun,
No more he'll twist the pussy's tail and make it yowl
   for fun,
The pussy's tail now stands out straight,
The gun is laid aside,
The monkey doesn't jump around since little Willie
   died.

Mr Carwynne liked to talk about the Crystal Palace. He
said that there was no place like it for amusement and
instruction anywhere near London, and he said people would
miss it if it was ever closed down or if it got burnt down.
He said that the most amusing exhibit was the Wurtemburg
Collection of Stuffed Animals and what a pity it was that
they were tucked away in the North Gallery instead of being
put in the Central Transept where more people would see
them. He was glad when I told him that I had found them
and how I laughed. He said that the man who arranged them
must have spent years over it, and what a humorous man he
must have been to arrange the little stuffed things in such
laughable situations.

I'm afraid that the moth may have got in 'em now and
they are no longer on show, but if you missed seeing them
when you went to the Palace, I will tell you about some of
them like I did to those little Jewish girls.

The animals were all small things such as moles, squirrels,
weasels, rats, small rabbits, cats and kittens, toads and long-
legged frogs. They were so well preserved that they looked
alive. The funny part was that they were all dressed up with
hats or bonnets on and tiny suits of clothes. They were
arranged in compartments like the inside of a house with the

animals sitting around and doing things like human beings do.

One scene was a farmhouse kitchen with a table and chairs, an old oak dresser and little brass candlesticks on the mantel. Little kittens sat at the table having breakfast. Some were boys and three were girls in white pinnies. A grown-up cat sat at the end pouring out coffee, and on one side of the fireplace an old grandfather cat reading a tiny newspaper sat opposite an old lady cat who was mending a stocking.

Another compartment was a big room in an inn with animals sitting about drinking or smoking long pipes. At a table in one corner four moles were playing cards, while a squirrel dressed as a waitress carried round drinks. It was funny to see her long tail sticking up through a hole at the back of her dress.

Then there was an inside of a church with a little white rabbit being married to a brown one by a monkey parson. Lots of other white rabbits sat on the side where the bride stood, and brown ones on the other side. Many of them were staring across at each other instead of attending to the ceremony.

Best of all was a duel between two large frogs who were standing on their long hind legs and fighting with swords. A crowd of all sorts of little animals stood around looking over each other's shoulders and looking excited, some weasels and monkeys had climbed trees to get a better view, and mice sat in a long row on the garden wall.

If you did see this collection, I am sure you came away wondering at the patience and ingenuity of the man who arranged it all.

Now I will tell you how I left Mr Carwynne and went into the grocery trade. I had thought of doing so for a long time, but something kept holding me back and I put off giving notice for a long time. One thing was that Mrs Carwynne was upstairs ill, so I had to stop until she was well again. I couldn't leave without seeing her – perhaps I should never see her any more. But after a few weeks, she came down looking quite well and brought a new little baby girl with her. She showed it to me and let me hold it, and then said they were going to name her Nellie, and 'when she grows up she will be a nice little wife for you, Tom'.

I didn't say so, but I didn't think much of that prospect — not waiting twenty years, I mean. Another thing, I'd rather have had Nellie's mother if she hadn't been married already. But I made a fuss of the baby just the same, and Mrs Carwynne kept that joke up for a long time. If she was in the back room and somebody wanted her in the shop she'd call me and say, 'Here, Tom. Just look after your wife for a minute,' and I'd go back and nurse it on my lap. The little thing was quite good with me, and it was wonderful to watch her growing bigger and prettier, and yet all she lived on was condensed milk. I used to get two tins of that every week when I went for the other grocery. I did all that sort of shopping for them.

Mrs Carwynne never ordered me to do anything. She would say, 'Would you like to go to the butcher's for me, Tom?' or 'Do you mind getting these things from the green-grocer?' She always spoke to me as if I was a gentleman instead of just their shop boy. So you see, it was hard for me to leave them and perhaps never see the nice lady and little Charley or the Nellie baby again.

One day I got bold enough to ask Mr Carwynne about prospects in the toy and fancy goods trade. He was quite reasonable and there wasn't much hope for a young fellow unless he had enough money to be an importer, and even then there wasn't a lot in it. The only ones he knew that had done a bit of good for themselves were those who had gone bankrupt once or twice, or had had fires!

Then I asked him if he'd mind me giving notice to leave as I wanted to go in the grocery trade. He said, 'Very well, Tom, and I wish you luck.' Mrs Carwynne wasn't so agreeable. She seemed to think that things would go on just as they were for ever. She came and asked me if I had been offended in any way, and then said, 'We haven't been unkind to you, Tom, have we?'

I tried to answer, but I felt that if I did I should go all sniffy again.

All I knew about grocery was what I remembered of our old shop years and years ago. But I hoped to get a situation as a sort of learner or improver and ask very small wages to start with. The best way would be to work at some shop for a few months and learn all one could there, and then go to another and pick up a bit more of the trade there. Because I was cheap, I had no trouble in getting taken on at the first place, and after a few months there I worked at seven different grocers' shops in about two years and noticed all the different ways they had of doing business. All of them were the same as regards hard work and long hours, though.

The first shop was in Bethnal Green in East London where I had board and lodging and sixteen pounds a year wages. The assistants were given a shilling a week 'beer money' as well, and that just about paid for my washing. Why they paid beer money was because years before all the fellows were given two glasses of 'table' beer a day, but later on many of them who had signed the Pledge and joined the Band of Hope when they were young thought it was unfair that some should have beer while all they had was water. So the finish of it was that the employers stopped the beer and gave money instead. The assistants didn't mind at all, as the beer was never up to much.

We opened shop at 7.30 and closed at 9, except on Friday and Saturday, when we kept open until 11 and 12. On the first four evenings in the week we could (after having some bread and cheese supper) go out until eleven o'clock, but if we weren't back punctually, we would be locked out. We had all Sunday free, so that was something. We went in to breakfast at eight and had cups of coffee and chunks of very stale bread and butter. That had to do until one o'clock dinner. But like all grocers, they sold biscuits. The Chief Assistant, who wore a Temperance blue ribbon in his buttonhole, and also a white silk one which meant some other sort of goodness, used to do some of the buying when travellers called, and he always ordered two tins of Huntley & Palmers Sponge Rusks every week, but I never saw any of those expensive biscuits sold all the time I was there.

Beside the manager, there were four assistants at that shop and all of them had come up from country places and worked for less wages than London fellows wanted. Sometimes when they had written and engaged a youth, his parents would back out at the last moment and refuse to let him come. They had read *Oliver Twist*, I expect, and remembered that Fagin and Bill Sikes had lived in Bethnal Green, so they thought it wasn't a nice place to send their sons to. I didn't find it much different from any other working-class district.

Most of the people were quite decent and respectable, except on Saturday nights, while as for 'Artful Dodgers', there were no more of those there than there are in the City — perhaps not so many.

Every morning we had to weigh and wrap up hundreds of pounds and half-pounds of sugar and other goods ready for Saturday's trade, and every afternoon except Friday and Saturday I had the job of chopping sugar. It was an awfully monotonous job, but I got to like it after a time, because while you were doing it you were free to go on thinking without interruption for three hours.

You chopped the loaf sugar with a heavy cutter which was slung by a strap to a spring behind it. The blade swung easily up and down and with your thumb on the top of the handle and one finger underneath, you kept it going — chump — chump — chump up and down, while with your free hand you fed the large pieces of sugar under the cutter until you had reduced them to the proper size for the family sugar basin.

All the lump sugar came from France. Some was in large cones weighing about twenty-two pounds, they were called 'loaves'. Another and heavier sort was called 'Titlers'. They were cone-shaped too, but the top end was left flat like a pedestal. These were made by Lebandy's in France, while the cones came from a firm named 'Say's'. I heard that Lebandy's were very wealthy and some of the partners were millionaires. One of them who was the richest suddenly got the idea to buy all the Sahara and reign there as Emperor, making Timbuctoo his capital. But his relatives and heirs got to hear about it, so they called in a few doctors and got him put away.

When you became an expert, you could chop up three sugar loaves in an hour, or ten in an afternoon. First you had to unwrap them and save the thick blue paper (that was sold to local doll-makers for making papier maché dolls' heads). Then the string had to be carefully rolled up in little balls — there were buyers for that too. There was a little ridge in the side of the sugar loaf; you laid a small chopper on this and gave it a blow with a mallet and so split the cone clean in half. Then a few more blows and the halves were reduced to sizeable pieces ready for the machine. Then your hands worked like a machine too and you could go on thinking, every now and then popping a lump of sugar in your mouth.

'That chap Lebandy. Fancy making all that money out of sugar. Ten hundred thousand pounds. Old Mr Gaynibb would have been more worried than ever trying to hold that lot, a million of money. Perhaps having too much is as much worry as having too little. Wish I had a lot. If I had a hundred pounds! Wonder how long it will take to save that. Sixteen pounds a year! How much is that a week? Say six bob — save half of that easy. Yes. Learn all I can here and then shift to a better-paid job. Save more then. Get in a nicer shop where you can talk to customers like Mrs Carwynne did. If you said, "Thank you *so* much" to Bethnal Green people they'd think you were "getting at them". They'd say, "Not *so* much of it." I'll go down the cellar every night after we shut and practice wrapping up packets of tea and things. Better than prowling round dingy streets for an hour. I may get to be better than any of them at wrapping up parcels. Yes, I'll do that. Wonder why I like the grocery trade better than all those other trades I've been in? Harder work than any of them. Perhaps it's the smell of grocers' shops, or the eatable things they sell. That chap Mosscrop with the blue ribbon said it isn't stealing if you eat a biscuit now and then or pop a raisin or a bit of candied peel in your mouth when you're weighing up. But if you took a pocket-full when you went out at night it would be. What you eat in the shop is food and they are supposed to provide you with food — it's part of your wages. Perhaps he's right. He ought to know. He goes to church Sundays and teaches Sunday School. . . . Bits of bacon rind in that stew we had for dinner to-day . . . (chop-chop, chop-chop, chop-chop). If I had a hundred pounds! I know why this shop smells nicer on Monday mornings. Being shut up all day Sunday the smells get all mixed up and shut in. A sweety spicy sort of smell. Sugar and spice, and all that's nice, that's what little girls are made of. . . . Chemists' shops smell of scented soap. Boot shops smell of leather. But a grocer's shop has heaps of smells all mixed up together. Better. Wish I could make poetry to go with this chop, chop, chopping. Mr Tennyson would. Like he did about the sea. "Break, break, break, on the cold grey stones, O sea." Chop, chop, chop into cold white cubes, O sugar. No, silly. . . . That beautiful song Lord Byron wrote. "I'll sing thee songs of Araby, and tales of far Cathay." Wonder where far Cathay is? Araby's where the coffee comes from.

> Oh! scents of Araby, coffee and tea,
> With a chump and a chop and a chop, chop, chop,
> Nothing is half so sweet to me
> As the smell of a grocer's shop, chop, chop.

No, mouldy — nothing like Tennyson's "O sea". . . .

'There weren't any cold grey stones on Swansea beach, only lovely sands. Wish I was there. Not to stop, I mean, just to have a few swims. What a lot of things have happened since I left Swansea! Thoughts and wishes and silly dreams, and schemes that came unstuck. Pigs and parrots, and pots of paint. Hampers of "things" on a truck. . . .

'When I get a hundred pounds I'll open a little grocer's shop in a side street. Do all the work myself. No more bosses over me. A shop with a little room behind where one could go and have a cup of tea and keep an eye on the shop. Wonder what's the time . . . wish I could see the shop clock from here. Must be near tea time. . . . If I get a shop like that I'd want a wife to help me and look after the house and all that. That little Fanny Topknot! She'd be the only one — you couldn't help being happy then. It would be fine. Perhaps when I'd opened the shop in the morning and dusted up a bit, she would open the parlour door and say, "Your breakfast is ready, Tom," (she might say "Tom dear") and I would answer, "Thank you, Fanny darling."

'But perhaps it wouldn't last like that and after a time it would be, "Now then, how much longer are you going to be? Your bloater's getting cold," and I might say, "All right, all right. Don't make a song about it." Oh, no, no. It wouldn't be like that, ever, not with little Fanny. Perhaps after a time we might have a little baby girl like Mrs Carwynne's Nellie. I should like that.

'Now they're going in to tea, so I must unhitch the spring-strap of the cutter and go in too. I can do with a cup . . . .'

Sometimes local publicans would order some loaf sugar cut very small. This was called 'Bar Lump'. It was put on the bar in the public houses for customers to help themselves and put a lump or two in their glass of spirits when they were having a drop with hot water in it. The sugar had to be cut to the size of dice and if you didn't watch out your fingers copped it properly. It took three times as long to chop, but it was charged a ha'penny a pound more, so it paid well compared with sugar generally.

Most grocers were lucky if they got a shilling a hundred-weight profit. The profits were cut down so by competition. They did it to attract customers to buy tea, on which they got quite a large profit. The grocers watched each other and the news would soon go round if Noggins or So-and-So had marked his sugar down by a farthing, and so it went on, one against the other.

One thing they did all agree about was to keep up a standard price for tea — tea was the great stand-by. It would have been suicide to start cutting prices of that. Many grocers wouldn't serve you with sugar only — you had to buy tea as well or some other profitable line. Our cheapest tea was 1s 6d a pound, but we sold most of the mixtures at 2s and 2s 6d. Some richer customers paid 3s a pound. When the customers asked for half a pound or so of tea, you asked them if they wanted it black or mixed. The tea we called mixed had about one fourth green tea blended with it, curly little leaves called 'gunpowder' tea. It came from China like most teas did, and it gave the tea a lot of flavour. All the old ladies bought the mixed tea. I found out that years ago everybody who drank tea bought the green as well as the black, and that's why you see two compartments in the old mahogany tea caddies.

Some grocers made up fancy names for their teas and if a grocer stuck bills on his windows it was always something about his wonderful tea. While I was thinking of this I was reminded of something — I wonder whether you ever heard of the 'Cannibal' tea at Kew Gardens? Many houses near the gardens supplied teas to visitors and one of them had a notice stuck up: 'Plain teas, 6d. With shrimps, 9d. With children, 1s.'

One grocer named Thomas Means had several shops about East London and one quite near us, and instead of just putting his name over the shop like most do, he put: 'T MEANS TEA.' I thought that was smart of him. Wish I had a name to fit in like that when I have a shop.

I only stopped at that Bethnal Green shop for four months, and by that time I thought I'd learned enough to be able to get something better. The other assistants were all very friendly and the manager a real good sort. He took his share in the work as much as any of us. He blended the tea in the cellar and carried it up in white sacks to fill the bins behind the counter. He was always free and easy with all of us, and chaffing or joking and taking a joke on himself. His name was Frostick and the older assistants called him 'Tick'. He didn't mind a bit. Yet in spite of all that he kept good order and the chaps were loyal and took no liberties.

The owner of the shop lived right away in north London. He owned several more shops and used to drive round and visit each one weekly to check the accounts and see that the takings had been banked. They never told me when I was engaged that our wages were paid quarterly, like servants' wages are, and yet we could leave or get the sack at a week's notice. None of the assistants thought it fair and Mosscrop said he did it so as to get interest on our money from the bank. He expected the men to be honest even though they had open tills and could have helped themselves. But I don't believe any of them did. The way they'd been brought up, I expect. A biscuit or two perhaps, but not real stealing.

A new assistant who perhaps had been out of work for several weeks would have very little money in his pocket to carry on for three months and when his first quarter's wages came there might be many things to buy — shirts, aprons or boots, or a new waistcoat — we always wore our waistcoats out first because we never wore our coats in the shop, we were always in our white shirt sleeves and our white apron kept our trousers clean. The waistcoat, being unprotected, soon got dirty and worn.

Soon after I had my first quarter's wages, four pounds all at once. I gave notice to leave and went back to Peckham. My landlady, Mrs Pagles, hadn't let my room. She seemed pleased to see me and I was glad to see her and the baby again.

I was glad too when the last Saturday night came at the Bethnal Green shop. We were supposed to shut at twelve on Saturday nights, but we never did because there was a large public house called 'The Green Gates' quite near, and when they closed at twelve lots of women came to our shop for their groceries and we were busy serving until half past twelve. Then by the time we'd got the shutters up it'd be quarter to one and the four of us would go into the back room and have a cup of cocoa. We took some of the best cocoa out of the shop and boiled the water on a gas ring. The manager and his wife and the servant had gone to bed at eleven and left us to it. We'd been on the go since half past seven in the morning with two short rests when we went in to dinner and tea, so we were glad to crawl up to bed on our aching feet. We slept in a large room two in each bed, and just as we had laid down we'd hear the church clock strike one, and Mosscrop always said, 'Did you ever hear it strike less than that, Tom?'

14

On looking back, I find that I haven't told you about the
only funny thing that happened while I was at that shop.
It was the first time I'd heard a lady swear. She was a fat big
girl and very pretty, and while she was looking at things in
our shop window one heel of her boots got wedged in our
cellar grating, and try as she would she couldn't get it out.
Some children got around and one little girl came to the door
and called out, 'Hi, mister. There's a lady jammed in your
grating.' So we went out and had a look. She was nice, but it
spoilt it a bit, her being so cross and swearing. She'd got on
those long button boots with high thin heels, and one of
them had gone right down between the gratings and was
fixed ever so tight. Our manager said she'd better unbutton
her boot and get her foot out. When she'd done that two of
our chaps helped her to hop into the shop and got her to sit
down. Then I had to go down the cellar and knock the boot
up with a bit of wood and a hammer. While I was doing that
I disturbed the dirt and rubbish underneath the grating and
found a fine pocket knife with a tortoiseshell handle, and a
mouldy penny.

When I went up she was looking at her boot and going on
about the heel being scratched and dented, as if it was our
fault. I told her that I knew all about boots and if she bought
a penny 'heel-ball' and melted it a bit and rubbed it on while
it was hot the dents wouldn't show. Then I asked if I could
put the boot on for her, and I did and buttoned it all the way

up. She never thanked me but looked cross all the time and said, 'What the hell are you laughing at?'

Every night after that, when I went down the cellar to practise wrapping things, I searched through all the dirt under that grating. It was about four inches deep with sawdust, rubbish, and road dust. I scraped it over and sifted it bit by bit and found over four shillings and sixpence in coppers and silver coins. Some had gone all green and many of the silver ones were black, and some had King George III on them.

I didn't tell anybody, but thought about it a good deal when I was chopping the sugar: 'Lots of money down cellar gratings all over London — very likely hundreds of pounds — might find half sovereigns in some of 'em. If you look down gratings outside shops there's always a lot of dirt on the bricks underneath. . . . Wonder if I could get at it? Go about and find empty shops with TO LET on them, get the key from the landlord . . . have to take a cinder sifter — and a coal shovel. Don't suppose they'd let me have the key — have to be an older person. No. What about going in shops and asking if you can clear all the dirt away and leave it nice and clean. Offer 'em sixpence if they'll let me do it. No — they'd get suspicious and tumble to it. Dress up dirty and say you're out of work and will do it for fourpence, no, tuppence. Perhaps they'd make it fourpence if you made a good job of it. Take an old overcoat with big pockets. A gold mine! No, you couldn't take a sifter, they'd smell a rat. Have to go through the dirt with your fingers. If there was four and six in our cellar, other gratings would have money down 'em too. People wouldn't have just picked on our grating to drop money down! Might find other things — a diamond ring worth lots of money. Couldn't pawn it though, want to know where I got it . . . might get locked up. Hide it. Give it to Fanny Topknot some day, if ever I find her. Don't suppose I ever shall. If I did she'd be too rich to look at me . . . unless I got rich too, by scraping under gratings. That old man in *Our Mutual Friend* got rich out of dustbin rubbish and things he found in it. The Golden Dustman — good mind to have a

154

go at it if I don't get work in another grocer's shop soon. If I do get another situation, I'll go and clean up under their grating first chance. . . .'

After three weeks tramping about after advertised jobs, I got engaged as a junior assistant by a grocer in Walworth Road. Following that, I went to one in Bermondsey and after that to Camberwell, staying a month or two at each. They were all cheap shops and you could not learn anything fresh at any of them. I had to take that or nothing because it was hard to get into a good class shop. They were very particular and if you hadn't been apprenticed they wouldn't look at you. But at last I did manage to get into one shop that was a cut above the others, a very busy shop in Southwark nearly opposite the South London Music Hall.

Besides the manager there were three assistants and an errand boy. I was called the 'third hand', and the errand boy and I did most of the hard work, but I also served lots of customers on Fridays and Saturdays. The one who was 'first hand' was older than any of us but he never bossed over the others and he got very friendly with me. We used to talk about books in our bedroom at night where we all slept in a large room. He wasn't like the rest of us, he was well educated and I wondered why he had come down to working in a shop like that instead of a better class one. His name was Biblowe, but we called him Bibby. Although we were so tired at night, we had some long talks in the dark after we'd gone to bed. He seemed to know all about everything and had read all the books any of us mentioned and lots more. I've just remembered that I lent him a book called *Under a Cloud* by James Greenwood and never got it back. I don't suppose I ever will now.

Some nights he burnt the candle all away while he was studying a book about journalism. He wanted to learn all about that so as to be able to write books and things some day and get out of shop life. He told me that he would have gone for a soldier, but his mother who was a widow begged him not to. He was good to his mother — he sent her best

part of his wages every month because she was poor and too
ill to work. Although he worked better than any of us, he
hated the trade and cursed the day he'd been put in it, saying
he'd 'rather sweep crossings'.

If he had gone in the army he'd have had to get up sharper
in the morning. He was always getting into trouble about
that. He wouldn't get up till the last thing, and we'd finished
washing before he made a move. He ought to have gone to
sleep earlier instead of talking and reading at night after
working like we did for so many hours. Some Saturday nights
when we went to bed soon after twelve, my arms ached so
that I could hardly unbutton my collar at the back. What
made the arms ache most was weighing up sugar. We had to
weigh up about five hundred pound packets every morning
besides lots of others up to six pounds in weight. This was
done in 'hand' scales, like you see the figure of Justice
holding. This meant that the scales weight and the sugar
had to be lifted up by your left hand several times before you
got the correct balance. One assistant filled the bags, another
weighed them and the chief assistant wrapped them up. You
soon got used to it and your left arm got much stronger than
your right.

One night we were talking about the long hours that young
fellows and girls had to work in shops in London, and I told
Biblowe about Swansea shops, how they all closed at seven
and at one o'clock on Thursday afternoon. He was astonished
at that, but said London shops couldn't do the same because
it was such a big place and the shopkeepers couldn't get
together and agree to close earlier like they could in a
country town. He said that it wasn't the shopkeepers' fault,
most of them would have liked to shut earlier for their own
sakes, but they couldn't because of competition. Each one
kept open because the others did, and some didn't shut up
until later than his competitor so as to capture some of his
trade — going to the door and watching to see if so-and-so
was putting his shutters up. You couldn't blame the
customers — they knew that the shops would be open no

matter how long after tea-time they left their shopping. The shops wouldn't close while there was trade about, and so it went on from bad to worse.

On Saturday nights at that shop the trade would slack off between ten and eleven and then get quite brisk again until midnight. This was mainly due to the Music Hall opposite. At six o'clock you could see crowds waiting to go in, the women taking their shopping bags with them. Then when they turned out at eleven they'd start their Saturday night shopping. Biblowe said that things would never be any better unless there was an Act of Parliament to make shops shut at a certain hour. The shopkeepers would welcome it just as much as the assistants. They didn't want to work all those hours any more than the men did.

'You'd have to shut all the shops to do this, because if the Act only regulated the hours of work instead of closing the shops the Guv'nor would still have to keep at it and thousands of shopkeepers couldn't afford to keep relays of assistants,' Biblowe told us. Even if they could, they'd still have to stick in the shop themselves to superintend. But before you could get an Act of Parliament the whole lot of us would have to get together and agitate. Oceans of work would have to be done, he said. But it could be brought about and it was worth working for even if we never lived to see it. The customers wouldn't mind much as long as they knew where they were — the men customers might grumble because they were more thoughtless and selfish than women — some of them might kick up a fuss and write to the papers if they couldn't buy tobacco after eight o'clock. Very likely Biblowe said a lot more about it, but I went to sleep.

Although the hours were long, they were nothing compared to those we had to put in at Christmas time. From the end of November we had to keep on working until one in the morning of the following day. So then it came about that Saturday got to be the shortest day in the week. We didn't work overtime on that day, because if we did we'd be working on Sunday and that would be irreligious and couldn't be thought of.

But they made up for it by waking us up at four o'clock on Monday morning so as to put in 3½ hours' work before the shop opened. The boss banged a boot on the stairs until one of us answered. We had to put a wet flannel on Biblowe's face to wake him and when he found what the time was he actually started crying. We were cold and felt miserable but to see a grown man crying made us laugh, and that made him swear, but more at the firm than at us. He cursed Christmas, the Guv'nor, and all the blasted grocery trade. He was in such a beautiful sleep, he said, he'd see 'em in hell first – he wouldn't get up (sob) and he curled up under the bedclothes again.

We left him and went down, but he thought better of it soon after and came down half-dressed. Then we started weighing and wrapping five hundred packets of candied peel and all the time he was so vicious and snarly that we were scared of him and I never contradicted anything he said. When we went up to breakfast at eight he was still full of spite about everything. He said, 'I'll get my own back; a fat lot of profit they'll get out of my morning's work.' And neither did they, for when the boss was up at breakfast, Biblowe went in the warehouse where stock was kept and smashed three large jars of jam, dashing them one on top of the other in the dustbin. Then he said he would serve us the same if we told about it. I thought perhaps he *ought* to have gone in the army.

That lot of candied peel was only one of the items of the things we had to prepare ready for the rush in Christmas week. So many Christmas Club customers would come that week to spend the money on their card, and cart away the goods for their annual feed. There wouldn't be time to weigh up the things then, so we had to have all we could ready to hand over. They took a long time to serve too. Some would have as much as thirty shillings on their card. Even quite poor-looking people would have over a pound.

After they'd ordered their cake and pudding things, they'd

get you to put down two or three half pounds of tea and four pounds of sugar. Then it would be. 'How much does that lot come to, young man?' You would reckon up the list you had made and tell them that there was perhaps nineteen shillings' worth to come. Then they ordered another lot of tea and sugar, jars of jam and marmalade and a packet of cocoa. None of them ordered coffee, it was too much trouble to make.

Then they'd say, 'How much have I got left now?' and you'd cast up the items again and find that there was still 11s 6d unspent. So down would go another lot of tea and sugar and after that they got bewildered and finished up by spending the balance on anything you liked to suggest. They'd pay 2s 6d for a bottle of French plums, and order a large box of crackers and a bottle of ginger wine — that wouldn't hurt them, there wasn't any alcohol in it — and then if there was a shilling or two left, you recited your little piece like you did every Saturday: 'Anymustardpeppersalt-ricesagotapiocasoapsodastarchorbootblackingblacklead?' And some of those articles balanced the account and brought a sigh of relief to both parties. Then you said, 'Thank you *so* much, Madam. We'll send them first thing in the morning.' And Madam would say, 'Merry Christmas, young man,' and sail out like a duchess.

When the shutters went up on Christmas Eve we were all thankful that all that extra work was over and done with for another year. I don't think any of us looked forward to having much of a 'merry' time next day, we were too fagged. As for me, if anyone offered me figs or muscatels on Christmas day I would have shuddered. I was sick of the sight of them. The boss gave each of us a Christmas present of five shillings for which we tried to put on a look of surprise and gratitude. We'd worked about eighty-four hours unpaid overtime during December. (We did get some holidays though. We got two days during the year and in the summer we got four days right off, Monday to Friday morning. We had to be back on Friday for the week-end trade.)

159

We had to be on our best behaviour after Christmas. Customers were rather stocked up with tea and things, so trade slacked off and some grocers tried to save on the wages bill by reducing the staff until things got better. It was generally the most expensive 'hand' that had to go. The others were given a small rise and promoted and had to share the extra work between them until trade got better, when a new young assistant would be engaged to fill the lowest vacancy in the ranks. None of us wanted to be out of work so soon after Christmas — it was the worst possible time. One might be out months before getting another situation. Another thing was we wanted to share in the Christmas 'boxes' that the commercial travellers from the wholesale houses gave the assistants in their customers' shops. For quite a month after Christmas the first assistant would put it to the different travellers when they called. Some gave without the asking, as a regular thing, some five shillings and others half-a-crown. It was shared out at the end of January, about ten shillings each. The errand boy didn't get a look in. Biblowe said that he got plenty from customers who he'd taken goods to all the year, that most of them gave him a shilling or sixpence. I didn't tell him, but I remembered that I didn't get anything when I was an errand boy except tuppence once when an old gentleman came to the door to take the boots in that I was delivering.

Biblowe finally got into trouble. He had started to learn Pitman's shorthand, and as our candle gave such a poor light and was soon burnt out, he decided to buy a paraffin lamp. So while he and I were left in the shop one dinner time, he popped over the road to an oil shop and bought one. Just after he had gone the Guv'nor came down to get a paper he had left on his desk, and seeing me alone he waited until Biblowe returned, and gave him notice to leave. The shop was never to be left without at least two assistants in it. We were all sorry to lose Biblowe, and I hoped he would get into something better and by and by write books and get more money to help his poor mother.

The place didn't seem the same after he had gone and I thought about leaving too. I liked him because although he talked so much he would let me talk too, and listen patiently. Once I told him a lot about the jobs I had had in Swansea, the pawnbroker, the china shop, and the ships I had to take things to, and he said that I ought to write a book about it, and when I told him that I didn't know enough to write books — not knowing long words and where to put the commas and thingemebobs, he said, 'Never mind. Just write it out as you have been telling me. Just as if you were talking; never mind the commas, shove 'em here and there and chance it.' So I said I would have a shot at it some day, when I'd got plenty of time.

Soon after he left, a traveller told me of a vacancy in a good class grocery store at Greenwich where a larger variety of goods were kept and better wages paid. They sold wines and spirits, provisions, patent medicines and dozens of things that ordinary grocers didn't stock. One could learn more there. So on Sunday I went there and saw the manager, who engaged me.

Like all the other grocers, they provided bed, board and beer money, but there were bugs in the bedroom as well. It was a large old house with a big shop built out over what was once a long front garden. Three other assistants slept in the same room as me, two of us in each bed. Everything was quite clean and the beds were good, but at night the bugs came from goodness knows where. For some reason they didn't trouble me, but my bedfellow suffered a good deal. In the morning he would show me the marks on his neck and arms.

Soon after the candle was put out and we were just off to sleep they commenced operations. They parachuted down from the ceiling and you'd hear them drop 'plonk' on the pillow and then they'd take a short cut over my neck to my companion. If they started on him before he'd gone to sleep he would catch a good many. But killing bugs is not a nice job, so he used to throw them across on to the other chaps' bed. I helped him some nights and we transferred quite a lot. You could hear the other fellows squirming about and swearing, and our bed would shake as we laughed silently. Though I was glad that they never bit me, I couldn't help wondering why and felt a little hurt at being rejected as if I was something unclean, like pork to a Jew. But I would have been more hurt had they dined off me, so perhaps it was all for the best.

They gave us good dinners at that shop. We went in relays to meals. Breakfast was the usual cup of coffee and chunks of bread and butter, but the manager, his wife and children sat at the same table tucking in to eggs and bacon and toast. At ten we went up in turns to the 'bug department' and washed and brushed up for the day. We were not allowed to go to our room after that and there was no facility for washing hands for the rest of the day, and that's the reason why I didn't stop long at that shop.

It was a pity because it was a fine place to learn all branches of the trade. But dealing as they did in so many different things they didn't specialize in any particular item, so I didn't learn much more about tea and coffee than I already knew.

When I told the manager why I was leaving he said I must want a place made for me. He asked if they didn't mind, why should I? and pointed out that I could rub my hands on a duster or on the swab behind the provision counter.

Perhaps my leaving drew attention to it and later on they may have provided at least a pail of clean water and a towel, so that their assistants could wash their hands before going in to dinner. A Jew would have done so without the asking.

162

15

Now I'm going to tell you how by a lucky chance I went to Ely and how two other lucky happenings helped me to hear news of Fanny 'Topknot' Tingey.

One of the advantages of 'living-in' where you are employed, and perhaps the only one, is the few opportunities you get spend money. Most of the shop assistants that I came in touch with saved some of their wages however small their earnings were. When they got their month's money, a portion went at once into the Post Office bank. The errand boys, who always lived out, did the banking for us for a small reward. So when I left Greenwich I had quite a good reserve. This time I didn't have to take any job that came along, but could wait until a chance came to get into a good-class shop. I remembered some advice I once had about dressing well — 'A good appearance and plenty of cheek will get you anywhere' — so I took enough out of the bank to buy some very good clothes. I felt much better when I had them on and Mrs Pagles started called me Mr Lloyd instead of Tom. (Each time I was out of work I went back to my young landlady, and once when my old room was let she made up a bed in her parlour for me.)

I think that dressing up better helped because when I applied in answer to advertisements I generally got an interview, but there were so many taller and better looking applicants that all that happened was that they took my name and address and 'would let me know'. But perhaps the good appearance didn't work because I hadn't enough 'cheek' to go with it.

After spending the morning in taking trams or walking after jobs, I spent the rest of the day in the City News Rooms. This was a four-storey building in Ludgate Circus. You paid a penny admission and were a free member for the day. There was a room where all the London and provincial newspapers could be read; another room to sit and talk, write letters or play draughts; a place upstairs where tea, coffee and cakes were served quite cheaply; and at the top a room where you could wash and brush up. You had to go to that room early, for later on the roller-towel got very careworn. It was hard to find a dry spot.

There was always a crowd of unemployed clerks and shop assistants there jolly and nice to talk to when they first came, but after a week or two grumpy and despondent. Their chief worry was boots. They wore out so fast going long distances after vacancies. Some couldn't get their boots mended, it was the only pair they'd got. They used to go in the writing room and dab some of the ink over a crack where the sock showed through. When they got tired of playing draughts a little group would get together and talk, mostly about the last job they had and their last employer and what they'd like to do to him. They'd club together and spend sixpence on an ounce of Three Castles tobacco and a packet of cigarette papers. They made quite a lot of cigarettes with that, sharing them out equally and tossing up for it if an odd one was left.

Most of the fellows had originally come to London from country towns or villages and were keen to read their local newspaper, but I never heard of one of them wishing to go back to their town. London was the place — always something going on, plenty of free entertainment, museums and picture galleries, and old London relics in the Guildhall Museum.

To suit a different taste there was the Museum of the College of Surgeons at Lincoln's Inn Field. You signed your name in a book at the door and walked in. If you went there in the morning and spent a couple of hours, you came away wiser but you lost your appetite! You didn't seem to want any dinner and so you saved a bit that way.

At the City News Rooms I first saw the paper called the *Christian World*. It had a lot of good reading and a large number of advertisements for assistants in the drapery and grocery trade. Some of the fellows agreed that it was a good medium for getting 'cribs', but the jobs were mostly in country towns and as leaving London was unthinkable the paper didn't interest them. One chap said that the advertisers believed that if they engaged a young person through that paper they would get one who was religious and had no bad habits, and consequently would accept lower wages than a more worldly one would.

As I had been out of work rather a long time, I thought I would put an advertisement in that paper and perhaps get the employers to come to me instead of me tramping about to them. I spent a long time trying to say in six lines what a desirable youth I was. *I* didn't mind leaving London a bit.

On the Monday after the *Christian World* came out I had quite a lot of replies, all from country places. Some asked for more particulars and others wanted me to come and see them. One went so far as to offer to engage me right away, so I must have piled it on in that advertisement. Only one offered to pay my railway fare, and as that promised a day's outing on the cheap, I wrote and asked what day would suit them. They replied that Saturday was the quietest day in their town and I was to catch an early train at Liverpool Street station and book to Fenburton. So I dressed in my best, bought a pair of gloves, and with a few pounds in my pocket went off hopefully.

The shop was kept by an old gentleman who was very deaf, and all the assistance he had was what help his wife could give. It was wonderful how they managed because it seemed the best shop in the place and included a Post Office. The grocer's deafness made it necessary to get someone to

165

serve and assist generally, and gradually relieve him of most of the work and Post Office duties as well. They would pay me twenty-five pounds a year and I could live with them as one of the family. They hadn't had an assistant before but needed one now because customers grumbled at having to shout. Before accepting I thought I would see what the town was like, and what sort of place it was to spend Sundays in, so I asked if they would give me an hour to think it over while I went for a walk round.

It wasn't a town really, just a big village, one long street with a small market square half-way. The buildings were very old and crowded together down each side in a jumble of small cottages, large houses with brass plates and here and there a little shop. One cottage had a notice, 'TEAS PROVIDED' — a nice little place to sit and think things over — but the lady said it was too early and she 'eent' got any water until the children came out of school, but if I went to the inn opposite, Mrs Barnes would get me tea. The inn was a large double-fronted cottage. Each side of the wide passage there was a small room with benches, chairs and a long table. I couldn't see any bar. Someone was talking loudly in some back room, so I went in one of the rooms and rang a little bell that was on the table. But no one came and the woman's voice went on louder and louder as if she was scolding someone. Now and then I heard a girl say something, but she only got a word or two in. Then a man came in from the street and clumped down the passage, and a girl said, 'Hallo, Uncle.' He said, 'Afternoon, Ducks,' and 'What's all the talk?' Then the woman told him and she did sound angry and excited.

'It's them gells of mine and that Kuzzin Tom kept them out 'till past ten he did. The disgrace of it. It'll be all over the place tomorrow. I'll give him Kuzzin Tom — the varmint. Met my gells and took 'em to a concert at the Corn Exchange he did. All men there except my gells — him with grown-up gells of his own — taking them to a place like that. A lot of men singing all sorts of songs. Then he drives home in his

166

market cart with the three of 'em. The old Turk, tells 'em to say that he's sending me a pair of ducks. Half past ten, mind you, and the house closed and me waiting up. I'll give him ducks when I see him. Taking gells of mine to such a place. He wouldn't take his own ducks there — gells I mean, the stuck-up bits.' Then there was a lot more of it all over again. She was properly wound up. So I rang the bell again, louder this time and a nice-looking girl came and took my order. I didn't like to bother them to get tea, so I asked for a glass of mild ale and some bread and cheese.

While I was getting on with that, the girl stayed and rubbed up the chairs with a duster and said something about the weather while I thought about the job I was offered. But after I'd had some of the beer I began to talk too. You can't think much when there's a pretty girl fiddling about, so I asked her what the people did with themselves on Sundays. Then she left off dusting and sat down. She said that most of the people went to church or chapel, and in the evening the women went in each other's houses after church to talk, and the men came in here. The younger ones went for walks along the 'Forty Foot' or up the 'droves'. In the winter they went up to the level crossing and watched the trains flash by, and some who liked a long walk went to Ely.

I said, 'What, Ely in Cambridgeshire?' and she said that it was all Cambridgeshire there. Then she went on and told me that she and her sisters went there yesterday to see the sports and they met their mother's cousin who took them to the hotel and gave them a nice tea. After that he took them to the Corn Exchange where there was a concert and said that when it was over he'd drive them home. They were the only girls there and it wasn't a proper concert really, just a sing-song. All the men sang a funny song in turn. They enjoyed it anyway, and it was ever so late before Cousin Tom drove them home and him being fat they were all squeezed up in his cart. 'Mother was so cross that she went on about half the night and hasn't left off yet.'

167

I asked her if she knew anyone named Tingey in Ely. She didn't, but said there were several families of that name in Witchford about three miles off from Ely. Some were quite well off and others not so much. She might have told me a lot more — she seemed to like talking — but the woman called out, 'Anneee,' so she had to go.

I thought what a bit of luck that that lady at the cottage hadn't got any water. I would go to Ely and see what sort of place that was. I might get a job in a grocers there. So I went back and told the old deaf gentleman that I was almost certain to accept his kind offer but I was going to Ely to stay till Monday and would let him know then.

The first thing to do in Ely was to find a place to sleep, but there didn't seem to be any place except the big hotel next the cathedral. I was rather nervous going in such a swell place, but they were very pleasant and obliging and gave me a small bedroom at the back and never asked for any money in advance. I had a nice tea with eggs and then went in the cathedral and saw its beautiful painted ceiling.

The rest of Ely wasn't much; grass was growing in some of the streets. If the cathedral clock hadn't banged out the hours all night it would have been a good place for Rip van Winkle to have had his twenty years' nap. When I went to the dining room on Sunday morning there were a lot of very well dressed people having breakfast at separate tables. It wasn't a bit like Colepeter's coffee shop and I did feel shy and awkward.' The waiter, who was a kind looking fat old gentleman, gave me a table all to myself in a corner. It had a lovely white tablecloth and knives and forks like silver, and you never saw such a breakfast as that waiter brought me. A great tray with coffee and milk in silver jugs and a large dish of bacon, eggs and mushrooms, rolls of bread, toast and jam and marmalade.

When I looked round at the other people they all seemed to be looking at me. Especially two oldish ladies who were dressed in black silk with lace collars. They looked so curiously at me that I felt like a sparrow might if he'd got in a cage with a lot of canaries. I tried to behave properly, sitting up straight and not sticking my elbows out when I was using the knife and fork, but I soon spoiled the effect by upsetting a large cup of coffee all over the clean cloth and they all looked at me more than ever. I was afraid that I should have to pay for the damage, but the waiter said it didn't matter in the least and he changed the cloth for a clean one. Then I stuck a newspaper against the coffee pot and, hiding behind that, went on eating until all the others had left.

After breakfast I didn't feel like going for a walk, so I got a magazine off a side table and sat in an armchair reading. But that waiter kept dodging in and out. Twice he came and told me that there was a service at the cathedral. I think he wanted to get rid of me, but I just said thank you each time until I got tired of his fiddling about, so I borrowed a magazine and went into the cathedral garden. As I left, the waiter said that lunch would be at one, but I'd eaten enough to carry on until tea time, so I wasn't interested.

I sat in the garden behind the cathedral reading and listening to the singing inside. It was very peaceful there. I had the garden all to myself; many pretty birds came near and I wished I'd saved something from breakfast to throw to them. I must have gone to sleep, for quite soon I saw the people coming from church.

I took the magazine back to the hotel and walked about Ely until I saw a sign-post saying 'TO WITCHFORD'. I walked there slowly along a long flat road. All the country around was very flat, no hills and few trees. If you climbed on a heap of stones by the roadside, you could see across for miles.

Witchford was a long-street sort of village with a few big houses, a lot of cottages and a very old church. I walked right through and back again without meeting a soul and just as I was walking through for the second time a thunderstorm came on and I had to run for shelter under some elm trees outside a fine old white house that looked like a farm. The house spread right along the path behind the trees. It had several windows on the ground floor with pretty white curtains and one or two smaller ones peeping out from the thatched roof. The rain came down in torrents and I would have got very wet had not a nice-looking oldish lady opened the door of the house and invited me to shelter inside.

The door opened into a large room with old beams across the ceiling and although the weather was warm a good fire was burning. There were two pretty girls in the room and you could see that they were the lady's daughters. They gave me a chair and then we sat looking at each other until the lady started talking. After something about the weather she asked questions. She wasn't rudely inquisitive. It was just to make conversation. At the same time she wanted to know — like they do in villages — was I staying with anyone in Witchford? Did I come from Cambridge University? Young men from the colleges often came that way on Sundays. Did I know any one in Witchford? And had I seen the cathedral at Ely? I had to say no to all that except the cathedral. I told her I liked that very much and that I was staying at the Lamb Hotel. Then I told her that I had been to college in Berkshire and when I was there I knew someone named Tingey who came from Witchford. I didn't like to say it was a little girl, but let them think it was a school fellow.

They were very interested then and began to speculate about who it could have been. They knew everybody in Witchford; most of them were related to each other, cousin or something. They couldn't think of any boy Tingey who had been to a school farther off than Ely. What was his other name? they asked. I didn't know, only Tingey. Perhaps I'd made a mistake I told them. Then they said that one family of that name had left Witchford some years ago and gone to London. They had a lot of children. It might be one of them. I thought a bit and asked the lady if the Christian names of the children were as uncommon as their surname. She said, 'No. Just good old English names like Tom and Harry, Minnie and Florrie. The eldest girl's name was Fanny Anne.' When

I heard that I thought a little more. Then I asked if she knew what part of London they had gone to. I knew London well, I told them. 'Yes. I heard that they went to Peckham,' she said. When I heard that I didn't know what to say for a minute. Then I changed the subject and said that someone in London had told me that all Cambridgeshire girls were pretty — was that true? The lady said, 'You shouldn't believe all you hear,' so I looked at the girls and said, 'No. But seeing's believing.' I don't think that lady liked it much, but the girls laughed. They were pretty, dark sort of girls, better than Annie at the inn, although she was very nice too. I should have liked to have stopped there talking to those girls a little longer, but the rain had stopped so I had to 'thank the lady *so* much' and go.

The lady said that one of her sons was walking to Ely and it would be company if we went together, so I thanked her again. I was glad to have her son to walk back with. He was a tall dark gentleman and spoke nicely. We talked together all the way and it made the three miles to Ely seem shorter.

When we parted at Ely I walked around looking for some place where I could get tea. I didn't fancy having it in that hotel with all those swells staring. In a road called Fore Hill I saw a cottage with cards in the window, 'TEAS AND REFRESHMENTS' and also 'LODGINGS FOR SINGLE MEN'. It looked a nice clean house so I knocked. The lady who came to the door asked me to come in and after a little talk she made me some tea with bread and butter and cake and agreed that I could sleep there that night.

I went back to the hotel and paid my bill there. I didn't like to give that waiter any money for himself, he was so grand-looking and might be insulted, so I asked him if he would put this shilling in his little sister's money box. He said he would and laughed. Then I went in the cathedral and sat near the door looking at that ceiling and listening to the droning voice of the preacher in the distance. I wished I had found that cottage in Fore Hill before I went to the hotel. The lady there only charged me half-a-crown for the tea and

171

the room and breakfast next morning.

Before I went to sleep that night I tried to think out what I'd better do. 'If I take that job in Fenburton it would really be funny — me living down here and that little girl living at Peckham. It must be the same girl — uncommon name like that. While I was working at Peckham she was living down here — now it will be the other way about — funny. Better go back to Peckham. I might find her. It might turn out to be a good thing if I worked for that deaf grocer — I could learn Post Office work. Perhaps get that business for myself some day. Save up. But what to do on Sundays? Annie at the inn? Pretty name, Annie. She's pretty too — nice brown eyes. When she was telling me about Cousin Tom I thought I should like to hug her. She'd have to get in early at night because of her mother. Perhaps she'd get like her mother some day and nag like she did. But — those two nice girls at Witchford? Six miles away from Fenburton! No. I bet Fanny "Topknot" has grown up nicer than any of 'em. No, London's the place — always something going on there. In the winter down here? Watch trains go by. I was silly not to ask that lady what Mr Tingey's business was. Perhaps he's got a shop. Go about and look. Fancy her having two names, Fanny Anne. Fanny Anne Topknot — F. A. T. fat. Hope she isn't. Not too fat, I mean, just nice. Yes. Write to that old gentleman — sorry unable to come. He promised to pay my railway fare — can't ask him for it now. Shouldn't have the cheek. No. Go back tomorrow. Fanny Anne . . . .'

None of the Peckham grocers wanted assistants, so I had to go farther and farther afield and after a week or two I was lucky. An old-fashioned tea grocer's in High Street, Borough, twenty-six pounds a year and live in. A fine place to learn all about tea. They did a big tea trade, blending it themselves. Of course, they sold other things as well, like most grocers do, but tea was the main thing. People came from far and near for John Rose's tea.

This was the first shop I'd worked at that closed as early as eight every night except Friday and Saturday, when it was ten and eleven. Not so bad compared with the others. Besides the manager, there were three other assistants; the chief one got thirty-five pounds a year and the others a few pounds less each down to me. I was the lowest on the list, so besides serving customers I had to help do rough work in the warehouse — chop sugar, and open chests of tea for an old gentleman who came once a week to blend it. He liked to talk while he was mixing the tea and told me many things I hadn't known about it. He bought the tea too, tasting the samples using little white teapots and cups without handles, which I had to wash up afterwards. Sometimes he would let me taste them to see if I could pick out the best. In the best blends he used very expensive tea from Darjeeling, but for the cheap sorts just two parts of Indian tea to one part cheap China. The China tea gave the blend a flavour and toned down the strength of the Indian. They sold many fancy teas for flavouring. Two sorts were called Scented Orange Pekoe; one came from Canton in China, long twisty leaves as big as a match. They called this Spiderleg Pekoe in the trade. The other sort was from Foochow, a very small greenish brown leaf. The old gentleman told me that like green tea it hadn't been fermented and turned black like other teas are, but just dried over stoves and then piled in heaps with china oranges inserted here and there. The scent of the oranges went into the tea. Tea, being so dry, sucks up the moisture out of the air and any scent or flavour that may be near it. That's why tea must be kept tightly shut up in a tin. If it's left about in paper near coffee or soap or other smelly things in a cupboard, it will quickly take up the scent of those and be spoiled.

He told me too that different quality teas all came off the same plant. The small leaf buds picked off the top of the bush were the finest and most expensive, called 'Pekoe'. The larger leaves a little lower down were called 'Pekoe Souchong' and the largest coarser leaves farther down the plant were 'Souchong'. The Indian tea growers had taken these Chinese names to describe their tea too. He said that the Chinese people grow teas that are nicer than any to drink, but they don't export any of the finest kind. They keep that for their own use. So if you don't know a Mandarin or some other rich person in China who would send you a small box of it, you will never know how delicious a cup of tea can be — and you wouldn't need milk or sugar with it.

I was lucky to get into a shop like that where one could learn so much about tea, but that was not the only fortunate thing, for quite an amazing thing, luckier than ever for me, happened soon.

Opposite our shop was a large draper and ladies' dress shop, and during their dinner hours girls from that shop came over to buy biscuits for dessert or just to fill up. Most of them bought a penn'orth, but those who wanted ginger nuts had to spend tuppence; they were heavier and you didn't get many for a penny. The manager was generally at dinner when they came over, so sometimes we held quite a reception. They were a nice looking lot of girls and there'd be some competition among the fellows to be first in serving them, and I being a new hand didn't get many chances, but I used to look at them a lot. One of the girls was taller than the others and didn't giggle. I thought I had never before seen such a nice girl. She was fresher looking than the others and reminded me of someone who I had seen somewhere before or else had dreamt about. Each time while she was being served with ginger nuts I looked at her and she seemed to get nicer and nicer every day. But when I did get a chance to serve her I couldn't get her to talk. She was so distant and reserved that I couldn't say much more than good morning, nice day and thank you *so* much. None of the other girls were like that.

One of them that the other chaps used to call Darkie (not in front of her, of course) was all chaff and chatter. She wore an engagement ring and seemed very happy about it, giggling and dancing about like a grasshopper. But I think the other fellows liked to serve the taller one best. Even the manager would sometimes and he was a married man.

I wish I could describe that girl to you like the novelists do. All about her eyes and nose and things, but perhaps you wouldn't believe me if I did. But really and truly I do believe that if she had lived in King Ahasuerus' time Esther wouldn't have had an earthly chance.

The drapers closed at eight too, and those girls who were employed in the dress-making department trooped out on their way home soon after. None of them lived in as we did. By the time our shutters were put up and we'd had a wash and a tidy up it would be a quarter past. Then there was the bread and cheese supper, a portion put ready for us in the dining room, so by the time that was disposed of it would be half past eight before we were able to get out for the evening and return at a quarter to eleven.

It was difficult if any of us wanted to run across any of those girls unless it was arranged beforehand, and if a girl you liked wouldn't talk to you when you were serving her with ginger nuts how *could* you arrange anything? One of the fellows often left his supper uneaten so as to get out quickly, but he'd got a regular young lady. But I always wanted my bread and cheese, and the other assistant would always eat his and any that was left too. He always seemed to be hungry, having come from a situation in the country where they gave him more and better food than most London shops provided for their assistants.

He used to annoy us very much at meal times by talking about what they gave him at Haverhill. He said they always had 'luxuries' for breakfast — a bloater one day, and an egg or a rasher of bacon the next, and so on. They even had a second helping at dinner! But in spite of all that he said he often got hungry between meals. So he got over that difficulty by keeping in with the cook or housemaid. 'You'd be surprised what a sixpenny bottle of scent will do.' At his last job he gave one to the housemaid and after that she couldn't do enough for him. If she met him on the stairs when he went up to wash at ten o'clock, she would slip a lump of bread pudding in his hand, or sometimes a slice of cold meat pie. But they didn't always meet on the stairs, so she took to leaving the doing-up of his room until the last, so that she would be there when he came up and she could give him a bit of food. She did this several times until the Missis got a bit nosey and started prowling about on the watch. One morning they heard her coming so the girl took the slop pail and bunked off while he finished washing quickly and went down. Then the Missis went in his room and found a cold sausage on the dressing table. That's why he he had to leave that crib, and the poor girl got the push too.

One day when I was serving Darkie with a penn'orth of Osborne biscuits, I asked her about that silent girl. She giggled more than ever and told me that her name was Fanny Tingey and she lived at Peckham. When I heard that, Darkie must have thought me rude. I looked at her with my mouth open and forgot to take a penny for the biscuits. When she came in next day I asked her more questions and she told me that Miss Tingey wasn't engaged, she hadn't any use for boys and that sometimes she walked home down the Old Kent Road. If I liked she would detain Miss Tingey that evening, keep her talking by the tramstop and if I came along she'd say, 'How d'ye do,' or something. I agreed and told her she had got a nice kind loving heart. Then she hopped out, giggling.

I hurried up that night and got my best hat and gloves, wrapped my bread and cheese up and stuffed it in my pocket. I saw the two girls talking, and as I passed them Darkie smiled and said, 'Good evening,' so I stopped and said, 'What an unexpected pleasure.' Then I said that I was walking to Peckham and Darkie said, 'Miss Tingey is going there too. Why not walk together?' So Darkie caught her tram and we went along the Old Kent Road. We walked in silence for quite a long way. I couldn't think of what to say to start a conversation. Then I remembered about a farm boy who walked out with a girl for the first time and all he could think of to say to her was whether she liked cheese. So I asked Miss Tingey why she liked ginger nuts better than other biscuits, and she said that they reminded her of the ginger-bread she used to buy at the village feast when she lived in the country. She had a nice soft voice, like a lady. Then I said, 'Don't you come from Witchford?' She said, 'Yes,' and looked surprised. Then I told her that 'years ago I loved a little girl who I saw at a college in Berkshire. She came from Witchford and her name was Fanny.' Then she was more surprised than before. She remembered her holiday there and the boys in church. She used to look at them, sitting in a long row in the church with their hair cut so short. They made her think of the coconuts they used to stick up in a row at Witchford fair. Then I told her how I had gone to Ely to look for her and the fine old house where I sheltered at Witchford.

We seemed to be getting along fine, and I had never before noticed what a nice long road the Old Kent Road was and how pleasant it was to walk down it. We got talking about books and she said she liked Oliver Goldsmith's works. She had all those at home and she lived quite near the house where Goldsmith lived and wrote. I'd lived in Peckham all those years and never knew that Oliver Goldsmith had lived there. It took nearly an hour to get to the road where she lived, talking all the time as we went along. She was a good listener too. It was quite a nice road with large houses and trees down each side. She stopped at the corner and gave me her hand but I didn't shake it. I lifted it up and kissed it like the knights used to do. Then I stood and watched her as she tripped along home — how lovely she was.

I found out soon after that she didn't live in that road at all, but in one farther away and not so good, but if I had known it I would have been gladder still. She might not be any better off than I was — it'd be a fair match and we'd start level.

As I went off on my way back I felt a lot better. A street organ was playing. 'When other lips and other hearts.' That made me think of what the Duke said in *Twelfth Night*:

'If music be the food of love — play on.'

And that reminded me of the bread and cheese, so I got that out and nibbled it as I went on my way.

After that first walk something seemed to tell me that it would be my fault if everything didn't turn out all right. Every evening I hurried out, and by and by we got friendly enough to make appointments. Then things got nicer still and I spent Sunday evenings in Peckham. But all the time we were no more than just friends — just someone to walk out with and talk to. We did a lot of talking, at least I did. Nothing about love or other sloppy stuff but things like two boys might talk about. That girl was years younger than me and there'd be plenty of time later on to talk about love. But a little bit of it would creep in now and then like when we were talking about fate. I didn't believe in fate but I told her that I was her fate, that it had all been mapped out and arranged that we should meet and be friends. And no matter how she tried to get out of it, or how many other fellows she might meet and like, nothing would alter it. She was my first and would be my only sweetheart. I said, 'You can't wriggle out of that. There's no getting away from fate.' She was the one for me and I was the one for her and that's how it would finish. She'd see. I don't know whether she believed it or not, but she laughed a good deal and said, 'Yes. We shall see.'

Come to think of it, Fate's a handy thing to believe in. You can do all sorts of silly things and then blame it onto fate. If you were having an argument with a bloke and he wouldn't listen to reason, so you had to hit him over the head with a brick, that'd be his fate, and it'd be the police-man's fate to run you in and then the magistrate wouldn't listen to any excuse about it being fate; he'd give you a month and that'd be your fate.

Shakespeare wrote, 'There's a divinity that shapes our ends,' but somewhere else he said that 'there's a tide in the affairs of men which taken at the flood leads on to fortune.' That means that you mustn't miss a chance when it comes along. So if things depend on chance it can't be fate. You can't have it both ways. There's a lot in chance and luck but more in your own determination. If you make up your mind to get a thing, or do something, and stick to it, you'll come off all right, bar accident. I know that's right, because if you set about it you can teach yourself to wrap up grocery parcels better than any one else in the shop.

Being in love helps a lot too. You get more determined than ever to make yourself worth more money to your employer so that you can save more, get that hundred pounds, open a shop and then get married.

Mr and Mrs Tingey had nine children and that family, together with some of their old friends from Cambridgeshire who'd moved to Peckham, made quite a party on Christmas evening. The sons brought friends in and Fanny's boy-friend was invited. It was very jolly there, the front parlour and the back room being made into one by folding doors. Mr Tingey was a tall handsome man, upstanding and strong looking, like Longfellow's village blacksmith, and Mrs Tingey was quite a little lady. All the family were good looking and quite different in manners and ways from most Peckham people. I had never met such a nice family. There were six sons and three daughters. One of the girls was named Minnie, about thirteen years old. She was dark and slim and looked like turning out to be a Spanish sort of beauty like the pictures you see on Muscatel boxes in grocer's shops. She didn't mind a bit being kissed under the mistletoe. The youngest girl was Florrie, a darling little thing, sweet and pretty, with lips like ripe cherries.

The piano was kept going most of the time and nearly everyone had to give a song, whether they could sing or not. The sons' girl-friends favoured sentimental songs. They sang of what they'd like to do 'In the Gloaming', wherever that is. One asked, 'Won't You Buy My Pretty Flowers?' and another sang about everything being nicer 'When There's Love at Home'. There wasn't much room for dancing but they managed somehow; and the older ones had to get out of the way while they played 'Postman's Knock' and musical chairs. It was a very cold Christmas outside, but jolly nice and warm in there and I thought how miserable it must be for any poor souls who might be wandering about alone with no Christmas party to go to. Most of all I liked the chorus of Mr Tingey's song:

> Waste not — want not — This maxim I would teach.
> Your watchword be despatch, and practise what you preach.
> Never let your chances like the sunbeam pass you by —
> You'll never miss the water till the well runs dry.

Do you know I think that this would be a good time to end my rambling tale. All things come to an end and I must finish somewhere. I expect you are a bit tired of it too. Well, we've had a nice long talk — at least *I* have — and it's a long time since I've had a chance to talk so much without being interrupted. So if you have followed as far as this I congratulate you on being such a good listener, and thank you *so* much. I hope you will keep well and happy.

POSTSCRIPT

P.S. Just a minute. I wonder if you'd really like to know about what happened a little later? Just a brief summary? Yes? No? How I had the cheek to apply for a situation in a first-class tea grocer's shop in a town about twelve miles out on the Thames? They advertised for an assistant who had to be well educated, of good address and manners, *quick at figures*, experienced in the tea trade and able to attend on customers of the highest class. I was very conceited at being selected for that job, but I heard afterwards that I was the only one who applied. That advertisement must have seemed too exacting to other out-of-work assistants. Anyhow I got it, and a very good firm it was too and after a while I was promoted and made chief assistant. We sold tons of tea, more in a week than many grocers sold in a year and lots of it at three and eightpence a pound.

Then I might tell you how one Sunday morning I went up to St Giles church in Camberwell and met Fanny 'Topknot' there and we had a wedding. And how after some years I went into business for myself in quite a different trade and had two shops. I could tell you a lot more if I had room.

Well, I've tried as best I can to relate some of the funny things that happened at the many shops I worked in. Many things weren't so funny, but I have forgotten them. It's hard to find an amusing side in some cases but it's generally there if you look hard enough, and the more you can laugh at things the happier you get, and happiness is the main thing when all's said and done. So when all's said and done nothing remains to be said.